# SOUP

A collection of delicious easy-to-make recipes

## Contents

Text by Ruby Smith.

Originally published in 2009 by L&K Designs. This edition published in 2010 by Myriad Books Limited.

## Publishers Disclaimer

The recipes contained in this book are passed on in good faith but the publisher cannot be held responsible for any adverse results. Please be aware that certain recipes may contain nuts.

# Chilled Avocado Soup

Serves: 4
Preparation time: 15 minutes
Cooking time: 5 minutes
Chilling time: 60 minutes

## Ingredients

4 ripe Hass avocados
juice of 4 limes
2 cucumbers, peeled, seeds removed and roughly chopped
1 large onion, peeled and cut into quarters
30g fresh coriander, finely chopped
1 vegetable or chicken stock cube made up with 500ml boiling water, chilled

## Ingredients for croutons

25g butter
1 tbsp olive oil
fresly ground pepper
1/2 tsp paprika
3 slices white bread, cut into 5mm dice

## Method

1. Peel, halve and stone the avocados. Chop the flesh and place in a food processor with the lime juice, cucumber and onion. Process until smooth.

2. Rub this mixture through a sieve, then combine with the coriander and stock. Put in the fridge to chill for an hour.

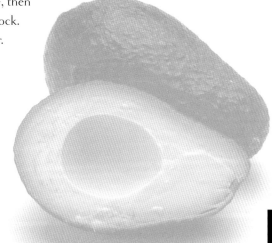

3. Heat the butter and oil in a frying pan. Combine the bread cubes with the seasoning and paprika, cook gently for 1-2 minutes until golden. Drain on absorbent kitchen paper. Serve the soup in individual bowls and top with croutons.

3

## Chilled Broad Bean and Pea Soup

Serves: 4
Preparation time: 10 minutes
Cooking time: 20 minutes
Chilling time: 120 minutes

### Ingredients

1kg broad beans in pods, or 350g frozen broad beans, thawed
500g peas in pods, or 250g frozen peas, thawed
25g margarine
1 large onion, finely chopped
900ml vegetable stock
2 sprigs of mint
150g carton of natural yogurt
1/4 tsp curry paste

### Method

1. Shell the beans and peas if they are fresh. Melt the margarine in a saucepan and gently fry the onion until softened.

2. Add the stock and bring back to the boil. Put in the beans, peas and mint sprigs. Cover and simmer for 20 minutes.

3. Remove the mint sprigs. Process the soup until smooth. Beat the yogurt with the curry paste. Add these to the soup and then blend again. Chill the soup for 2 hours.

## Broccoli and Lemon Gazpacho

Serves: 4
Preparation time: 20 minutes
Cooking time: 20 minutes
Chilling time: 60 minutes

### Ingredients

375g broccoli, cut into small pieces
25g butter
1 large onion, chopped
1 1/2 litres vegetable stock

1 lemon, de-seeded and cut into small cubes
10 large garlic cloves, chopped
450ml single cream
freshly ground black pepper

## Ingredients for garnish

strips of lemon zest

## Method

1. Reserve a few of the broccoli florets to garnish and lightly steam the rest. In order to retain colour and crispness do not overcook. Remove the broccoli from the pan and let it cool.

2. Melt the butter in a large saucepan over medium-low heat. Add the onion and fry until it begins to brown, stirring occasionally.

3. Add the broccoli, stock and lemon to the pan. Raise the heat until the soup barely simmers, turn the heat to low, cover and cook for 15 minutes, or until the lemon is soft.

4. Put the soup, in batches, through a food processor or blender, along with the uncooked garlic. Add the cream and pepper to taste. Cool and chill the soup for an hour.

5. Garnish the soup with the reserved broccoli florets and lemon zest strips to serve.

## Iced Crème Courgette Soup

Serves: 4
Preparation time: 10 minutes
Cooking time: 30 minutes
Chilling time: 60 minutes

### Ingredients

25g butter
500g courgettes, thinly sliced
750ml chicken stock
freshly ground black pepper
1/4 tsp dried Italian herbs
1/2 bunch watercress, stalks removed
150ml fresh soured cream
3 ice cubes crushed

### Method

1. Melt the butter in a saucepan. Add the courgettes and cook gently until tender. Stir in the stock, pepper and herbs. Reserve a few watercress sprigs for garnish and add the rest to the pan. Bring to the boil, then cover and simmer gently for 20 minutes.

2. Puree the soup in a liquidiser or rub through a sieve, then pour into a bowl. Cool, then cover and chill thoroughly for an hour.

3. Just before serving, stir in the soured cream. Serve garnished with crushed ice and the reserved watercress sprigs.

## Gazpacho

Serves: 2
Preparation time: 10 minutes
Chilling time: 120 minutes

### Ingredients

400g tin of chopped tomatoes
1/2 shallot, finely chopped
1/2 green pepper, de-seeded and finely chopped
1 clove garlic

2 tbsps olive oil
2 tsp red wine vinegar
1 lemon or lime
Cucumber and tomatoes to garnish

## Method

1. In a food processor, blitz the chopped tomatoes, the shallot, green pepper and garlic. Add the oil and red wine vinegar then process until smooth.

2. Place the mixture in a bowl and season with salt and freshly ground black pepper. Add the juice of the lemon or lime chill thoroughly in the fridge for several hours.

3. Top the soup with diced cucumber and de-seeded tomatoes and serve with crusty bread.

## Chilled Prawn and Cucumber Soup

Serves: 4
Preparation time: 75 minutes
Cooking time: 0 minutes
Chilling time: 60 minutes

### Ingredients for the soup

1/2 cucumber, chopped roughly
100g peeled prawns, thawed if frozen
450g carton of low fat natural yogurt
1 tsp lemon juice
1 tsp chopped fresh mint
2 tsps chopped fresh parsley
1 tsp chopped fresh chives
freshly ground black pepper

### Ingredients for garnish

30g chopped prawns
chopped chives

## Chilled Prawn and Cucumber Soup/cont.
### Method

1. Place the cucumber, prawns, yogurt and lemon juice in a blender or food processor and process until roughly chopped, but not too smooth.

2. Stir in the herbs and season to taste. Pour into individual dishes and chill thoroughly for about 1 hour. Serve garnished with a prawn and chives.

## Chilled Potato and Leek Soup

Serves: 4
Preparation time: 10 minutes
Cooking time: 25 minutes
Chilling time: 60 minutes

### Ingredients

350g new potatoes, scrubbed and sliced
2 tsps olive oil
2 leeks, washed and sliced
2 vegetable stock cubes
550ml water
450ml semi-skimmed milk
salt and black pepper
4 slices French bread
4 thin slices Welsh goat's cheese

### Method

1. Heat the oil in a large saucepan, add the leeks and fry gently for 3-4 minutes or until softened.

2. Add the new potatoes, stock cubes, water and milk and season to taste. Cover and simmer for 15-20 minutes until tender. Liquidise half the soup. Stir in the remaining soup and chill.

3. Meanwhile toast one side of the bread. Top the un-toasted side with goat's cheese and grill until golden. Serve the soup topped with toasted croutons and serve immediately.

# Chilled Watercress Soup with cheese croutons

Serves: 4
Preparation time: 25 minutes
Cooking time: 40 minutes
Freezing time: 120 minutes

## Ingredients

25g butter
1 shallot, chopped finely
1 leek, chopped finely
250g potato, chopped
2 bunches watercress, chopped roughly
600ml chicken stock
300ml milk
freshly ground black pepper to taste

## Ingredients for cheesy croutons

2 slices white bread, crusts removed
1 tsp made English mustard
50g matured Cheddar cheese, sliced

## Ingredients for garnish

4 tbsps double cream, lightly whipped

## Method

1. Melt the butter in a large saucepan, add the shallot and leek and cook for 2 minutes, stirring, without browning. Add the potato and cook for 5 minutes, stirring.

2. Add half the watercress, the stock, milk and seasoning. Bring slowly to the boil, then cover and simmer for 30 minutes. Remove from the heat and cool slightly. Puree in a blender or food processor, then chill.

3. Pour a few tbspfuls of the soup into an ice cube tray and freeze for 2 hours. Leave the remaining soup in the refrigerator. Pour the soup into 4 bowls, add some frozen soup to each and leave for 30 minutes, until melted. Stir the remaining watercress into the soup and swirl the cream on top.

4. Pour the soup into 4 bowls, add some frozen soup to each bowl and leave for 30 minutes, until melted. Stir the remaining watercress into the soup and swirl the cream on top

5. To make the croutons, toast the bread lightly on both sides. Spread with the mustard and top with the cheese. Place under a preheated hot grill for 2-3 minutes, until golden. Cut into squares and serve with the soup.

## Chilled Tomato and Rocket Pesto Soup
Serves: 6
Preparation time: 10 minutes plus overnight marinating
Chilling time: 8-12 hours

## Ingredients
1kg/2 1/4lb ripe tomatoes, roughly chopped
1 green pepper, deseeded and roughly chopped
1 onion, chopped
2 cloves garlic, crushed
3 tbsps wild rocket pesto
salt and freshly ground pepper

## Method
1. First place the tomatoes, green pepper, onion and garlic in a large bowl. Add 2 tbsp of pesto and mix thoroughly. Then leave to marinate overnight, or for at least 8 hours, to let the flavours combine and deepen.

2. The next day place the tomato mix into a processor and process until smooth and season with salt and pepper. Finally serve in bowls and drizzle with the remaining pesto.

## Oven Baked Bean Soup

Serves: 4
Preparation time: 45 minutes
Cooking time: 120 minute

### Ingredients

2 tbsps olive oil
4 garlic cloves, chopped
1 large onion, chopped
6 pork ribs
4-6 strips of pork belly, cubed finely, or 6-8 streaky pork rashers, chopped
400g can of chopped tomatoes
3 tbsps tomato purée
1 litre water, or meat or vegetable stock
375g dried borlotti beans, soaked overnight in cold water, or 2 x 432g can of borlotti beans, drained
freshly ground black pepper

### Ingredients for serving

6 slices coarse bread, such as ciabatta
1-2 small onions, sliced very finely
a handful of fresh basil leaves, shredded
freshly ground pepper

### Method

1. Preheat the oven to 180°C, 350°F, gas mark 4. Heat the oil in a large flameproof casserole and fry the garlic and onion for about 5 minutes or until soft but not brown.

2. Add the pork ribs and cubed pork belly or bacon and cook until brown on all sides. Add the tomatoes, tomato purée and stock. Stir carefully and season with pepper. Bring to the boil, then reduce the heat and simmer for about 20 minutes.

3. Meanwhile, if using soaked dried beans, drain them and put them in a saucepan. Cover with fresh water, bring to the boil and boil rapidly for 10 minutes. Drain and add to the casserole. Canned beans may be added without pre-boiling.

## Oven Baked Bean Soup/cont.

4. Transfer the soup to the oven and cook for 1-2 hours (if dried beans have been used) or until the beans are tender. If canned beans have been used, cook for about 1 hour.

5. Just before serving, toast the bread slices and arrange them in the bottom of a warmed wide serving bowl, or place them in individual soup bowls. Scatter the onion slices on top. Pour the soup over the bread. Grind some pepper over the soup, sprinkle with basil and serve immediately.

## Bacon and Parsnip Soup

Serves: 4
Preparation time: 15 minutes
Cooking time: 35 minutes

### Ingredients

25g butter
1 tbsp oil
1 onion, chopped
1 carrot, chopped
250g parsnips, chopped
250g cooked lean gammon or shoulder joint, 1cm diced
1 litre vegetable stock
freshly ground black pepper

### Ingredients for serving

freshly chopped parsley
a little single cream
croutons

### Method

1. Heat the butter and oil in a large pan. Add the onion, carrot and parsnip and cook gently for 5-6 minutes.

2. Add the gammon and stock and bring to the boil. Simmer gently for 25-30 minutes. Puree the soup until smooth and return to the pan. Add seasoning to taste and serve hot with croutons, a swirl of cream and freshly chopped parsley.

## *Brisket Scotch Broth Main Meal Soup*

Serves: 4

Preparation time: 10 minutes

Cooking time: 75 minutes

### Ingredients

25g butter

750g beef brisket joint

2 carrots, peeled

1 turnip peeled

1 leek, cleaned

100g pearl barley

2 beef stock cubes made up with 1 1/2 litres boiling water.

1 potato, peeled and chopped

1/2 savoy cabbage, sliced

freshly ground black pepper

### Method

1. In a very large pan, heat the butter and brown the brisket. Cut the carrot, turnip and leek into 4 pieces each, and when the meat is quite brown add the vegetables and pearl barley.

2. Pour on the stock and bring to the simmer - adjust the seasoning and cook for 1 hour. Add the potato and cabbage, and simmer for a further 15mins. Remove beef and slice thickly. Spoon the soup into bowls and top with the beef.

## *Spicy Leek Soup with Blue cheese*

Serves: 4

Preparation time: 10 minutes

Cooking time: 30 minutes

### Ingredients

500g potatoes, peeled and cubed

1 1/2 large leeks, shredded

1/2 tsp coriander seeds

1/2 tsp ground curry spices

1 litre vegetable stock

## Spicy Leek Soup with Blue cheese/cont.

### Ingredients

150ml milk

150g blue cheese, crumbled

### Method

1. Sauté the peeled and cubed potato and shredded leeks. Add the coriander seeds and the ground curry spices, cook for 2 minutes.

2. Add the vegetable stock, bring to the boil and simmer for 15-20 minutes. Purée, season and add the milk and the crumbled blue cheese.

## Spicy Marrow Soup

Serves: 4

Preparation time: 10 minutes

Cooking time: 15 minutes

### Ingredients

25g butter

1 tbsp oil

1 small onion, finely chopped

1 garlic clove, crushed

1 tbsp smoked paprika

1 tbsp tomato puree

1 marrow peeled, deseeded and cut into 2cm dice

1 vegetable stock cube made up with 600ml boiling water

400ml tin coconut milk

### Method

1. Heat the oil and butter in a large saucepan, then add the onions and cook over a moderate heat for 3-4 minutes or until softened. Then add the garlic, paprika and tomato puree and cook for a further minute. Add the marrow and stock and bring to the boil, then simmer for 10-12 minutes or until tender to the point of a knife.

2. Transfer to a liquidiser and process until smooth. Return to the rinsed saucepan, then add the coconut milk and gently heat through. Season accordingly. Serve with chunks of crusty bread.

## Spicy Red Pepper Soup

Serves: 4

Preparation time: 20 minutes

Cooking time: 30 minutes

### Ingredients

1 tbsp olive or sunflower oil

500g onions, sliced

250g potatoes, sliced

500g red peppers, de-seeded and chopped

1/2 tsp paprika

1/2 tsp chilli powder

750ml vegetable stock

150g carton of low fat yogurt

freshly ground black pepper

### Ingredients for garnish

chopped fresh chives, to garnish

### Method

1. Heat the oil in a large saucepan and gently cook the onions for 5-10 minutes, until softened. Add the potatoes, peppers, paprika, chilli powder, season and cook, stirring for 1 minute.

2. Stir in the stock and bring to the boil. Cover the pan and simmer for 25-30 minutes until tender, stirring occasionally.

3. Allow the soup to cool slightly, then process in a food processor or blender until smooth. Return to the pan and reheat gently. Check the seasoning. Swirl the yogurt through the soup. Garnish with the chopped chives.

## Curried Leek and Sweet Potato Soup

Serves: 4
Preparation time: 15 minutes
Cooking time: 45 minutes

### Ingredients

1 kg leeks, finely chopped in a food processor
1 kg sweet potato, peeled and finely chopped in a food processor
50g butter
1 tbsp olive oil
2 tsps ground turmeric
1 tsp each of ground clove, coriander, cumin, mild chilli and cardamom
sprinkling of ground sea salt and black pepper
1 1/2 pints vegetable stock
300ml single cream
50g fresh coriander leaf, finely chopped, leaving a few whole leaves for garnish

### Method

1. Gently sweat the shredded leek in the butter and olive oil for 5 minutes to soften. Stir in the spices and cook for a further 3 minutes. Add the sweet potato, seasoning and stock. Bring to a gentle simmer. Cover and simmer for 30 minutes.

2. Whiz in batches in a food processor with the single cream and coriander until smooth. Top with the coriander leaf and serve with fingers of warm naan bread.

## Spicy Carrot Soup

Serves: 4
Preparation time: 30 minutes
Cooking time: 20 minutes

### Ingredients

500g carrots, scraped
15g reduced fat margarine
1 medium-size onion, sliced thinly
1 clove of garlic, chopped finely

tsp paprika

 good pinch of chilli powder

)00ml vegetable stock

 tbsp tomato purée

## Method

. Finely grate 50g of the carrots. Thinly slice the rest. Melt the butter or margarine
 n a saucepan on a low heat. Stir in the sliced carrots, onion, garlic, paprika and
:hilli powder.

2. Cover the pan and cook on a very low heat for 10 minutes. Pour in the stock and
 idd the tomato purée. Bring the soup to the boil, cover and simmer for 20 minutes.

3. Either process the soup in a blender or food processor or push through a sieve.
Return it to the saucepan and reheat if necessary. Serve in individual bowls, with the
 grated carrot floating on top.

## Celeriac, Carrot and Chilli Soup

Serves: 6-8

Preparation time: 15 minutes

Cooking time: 25 minutes

## Ingredients

 tsp olive oil

2 medium onions, finely chopped

 clove garlic, finely chopped

 red chilli, deseeded and finely chopped, optional

 celeriac, peeled and diced

500g carrots, peeled and diced

250g celery, sliced

2 vegetable stock cubes

 reshly ground black pepper

## Ingredients for serving

 5g pack fresh coriander

## Celeriac, Carrot and Chilli Soup/cont.
### Method

1. Heat the oil in a large saucepan and cook the onion until softened. Add the garlic and red chilli and cook for a further minute.

2. Combine the vegetables and add to the saucepan, allowing them to cook for a few minutes before adding the vegetable stock and half of the fresh coriander.

3. Bring to the boil, reduce the heat, partially cover with a lid and allow to simmer for 25 minutes. Liquidise or blend the soup in a processor until smooth. Return the soup to a clean saucepan, season to taste and warm through before serving, sprinkled with coriander.

## Spicy Tomato Chowder

Serves: 4-6
Preparation time: 20 mins
Cooking time: 30 mins

### Ingredients

1 tbsp vegetable oil
1 onion, chopped
1 clove garlic, crushed
350g/12 oz potato, peeled and finely diced
2 x 400g/14 oz can chopped tomatoes
1 green pepper, deseeded and finely chopped
2 tsps chilli sauce
salt and freshly ground black pepper

### Method

1. Heat the oil in a large saucepan for 2 minutes. Add the onion and garlic and fry over a medium heat for 5 minutes. Add the potatoes, chopped tomatoes, pepper and chilli sauce and mix well with a wooden spoon.

2. Season to taste, cover and simmer for 20-25 minutes until the potato is cooked. If the soup is a little thick add a small amount of water. Remember to stir occasionally.

# Seafood Saffron Soup

Serves: 4

Preparation time: 15 minutes

Cooking time: 30 minutes

## Ingredients

2 large onions, chopped

250g potatoes, diced

600ml milk

300ml fish or chicken stock

750g white fish fillets

12 mussels still in the shells

4 shelled scallops roughly chopped

120ml white wine

1 tsp powdered saffron

freshly ground black pepper

125g peeled prawns

142ml double cream

few unshelled cooked prawns

## Method

1. Put the onions and potatoes in a pan, add the milk and stock and bring to the boil. Cook for 15 minutes, until soft. Cool slightly, then sieve or process until smooth.

2. Cut the fish into 4cm pieces. Return the soup to the pan and add the fish and scallops. Cook gently for about 10 minutes until tender. Stir in the wine and saffron and season with pepper to taste.

3. Stir in the prawns and cream and serve immediately, garnished with prawns and chopped parsley.

## Sweetcorn and Prawn Soup

Serves: 4
Preparation time: 5 minutes
Cooking time: 10 minutes

### Ingredients

2 tbsps finely chopped ginger root
1 tbsp dry sherry
100g peeled prawns
900ml chicken stock
326g can sweetcorn
200ml tub creme fraiche
50g lean ham, diced
1 tbsp chives, chopped
freshly ground black pepper

### Method

1. Mix the ginger, sherry and prawns together. Bring the stock to the boil, then stir in the prawn mixture. Drain the sweetcorn and add to the pan. Cook for 2 minutes, stirring occasionally.

2. Stir in creme fraiche, sprinkle with the ham and chives, season with freshly ground black pepper and serve immediately.

## Cream of Haddock Soup

Serves: 4
Preparation time: 10 minutes
Cooking time: 45 minutes

### Ingredients

50g butter
1 onion sliced
1 carrot sliced
1 celery stick sliced
bay leaf
6 peppercorns
lemon slice

80ml dry vermouth
700ml water
400g filleted haddock
2 tbsps plain flour
freshly ground black pepper

## Ingredients for serving

125g frozen prawns, thawed
4 tbsps single cream
chervil or parsley

## Method

1. Melt 15g of the butter in a large saucepan and saute the onion until soft. Add the carrot, celery, bay leaf, peppercorns, lemon, vermouth, water and seasoning to taste.

2. Bring to the boil, cover and simmer for 20 minutes. Strain. Poach the fish gently in 200ml of the stock for 10 minutes, then remove and cool.

3. Melt the remaining butter in a pan, stir in the flour and cook, stirring, for 2 to 3 minutes. Gradually stir in the remaining stock. Bring to the boil and simmer, uncovered for 10 minutes. Return the fish to the soup and puree in an electric blender or rub through a sieve.

4. Add the prawns, check the seasoning and simmer for a few minutes. Stir in the cream and garnish with chervil or parsley.

## Smoked Cod Chowder

Serves: 4
Preparation time: 10 minutes
Cooking time: 15 minutes

## Ingredients

350g smoked cod fillet, skinned
1 medium size onion, chopped
600ml skimmed milk
1 bay leaf

## Smoked Cod Chowder/cont.

### Ingredients

2 tsps cornflour

300ml water

198g can sweetcorn

1 tbsp chopped parsley

3 tbsps dry sherry

freshly ground black pepper

### Method

1. Poach the fish and chopped onion in the milk for 15 minutes, with a bay leaf for flavouring.

2. Break up the fish with a fork. Blend the cornflour with the water and add this to the soup. Bring it to the boil and simmer until slightly thickened.

3. Add the sweetcorn and parsley, and re-heat to just below boiling point. Just before serving add the sherry and season to taste.

## *Jerusalem Artichoke and Smoked Oyster Soup*

Serves: 4

Preparation time: 10 minutes

Cooking time: 30 minutes

### Ingredients

900g Jerusalem artichokes, peeled well and chopped

1 tbsp lemon juice

105g can smoked oysters in oil

25g butter

2 large cloves garlic, peeled

a little milk (optional)

150ml carton double cream

freshly ground black pepper

chopped parsley

## Method

1. Place the chopped Jerusalem artichoke in a saucepan and just cover with water. Add the lemon juice, the oil from the tin of oysters, the butter and the garlic cloves.

2. Simmer gently until the artichoke pieces are tender. Liquidise and sieve all the ingredients, together with the cooking water.

3. Taste the soup, adjust the seasoning and if necessary, thin out with a little milk.

4. Whip the cream and chop the smoked oysters. Add the oysters to the cream, together with as much chopped parsley as you like.

5. Serve the soup with mounds of this mixture spooned into the centre of each bowl.

## *Smoked Haddock and Sweetcorn Chowder*

Serves: 4
Preparation time: 5 minutes
Cooking time: 25 minutes

## Ingredients

2 celery sticks, finely sliced
1 large potato, peeled and diced
1 small onion, peeled and finely sliced
350ml water
400g pack Swiss fondue or thick cheese sauce
250ml milk
400g pack smoked haddock, cubed
3 rashers bacon, rind removed and chopped
198g can sweetcorn kernels, drained (optional)
15g pack parsley, finely chopped

## Method

1. In a large saucepan simmer the celery, potato and onion with the water for approximately 15 minutes or until tender.

## Smoked Haddock and Sweetcorn Chowder/cont.

2. Blend in the fondue and milk and cook until liquid like and smooth. Add the smoked haddock, bacon and sweetcorn, cook for 5-8 minutes. Finally add in the parsley. Serve immediately.

## Smoky Corn Chowder

Serves: 4
Preparation time: 30 minutes
Cooking time: 10 minutes

### Ingredients

25g butter
1 onion, thinly sliced
1 red pepper, cored, deseeded and thinly sliced
2 potatoes, diced
175g button mushrooms
25g plain flour
300ml milk
450ml stock
500g smoked haddock fillet
326g can sweetcorn kernels, drained
2 tbsps chopped parsley
freshly ground black pepper

### Method

1. Melt the butter in a large pan, add the onion, red pepper, potato and mushrooms and cook until the onion is soft.

2. Stir in the flour, then the milk and stock. Bring to the boil, stirring constantly. Remove any skin and bones from the haddock and chop the flesh into 2.5cm pieces. Add to the soup with the sweetcorn and pepper.

3. Simmer for 10 minutes, then stir in the parsley. Leave to cool.

# Chicken Soup

Serves: 4
Preparation time: 15 minutes
Cooking time: 2 hrs 10 min

## Ingredients

250ml olive oil
1 onion, finely chopped
2 carrots, finely chopped
4 celery sticks, thinly chopped
200g fresh spinach
1 garlic clove, crushed
2 chicken legs
250g cooked chickpeas
4 tbsps flaked almonds, toasted
1 pint chicken stock
1 pint water
1 bay leaf
1 tbsp parsley, finely chopped
salt and fresh ground black pepper
1 loaf Italian ciabatta

## Method

1. Heat the oil in a large saucepan and gently fry the vegetables and garlic until softened. Add the chicken legs and continue cooking until they are golden brown.

2. Stir in the chickpeas and the almonds. Pour in the stock, water and bay leaf and simmer covered for 2 hours.

3. Remove the legs and take off the skin. Shred the meat and return it to the pan.

4. Cut two slices from the ciabatta, break them into small pieces and add to the soup to thicken it.

5. Stir in the parsley and season to taste. Serve immediately, with the remaining ciabatta, toasted, cut into slices and rubbed with garlic.

## Spiced Beef Soup

Serves: 4
Preparation time: 10 minutes
Cooking time: 40 minutes

### Ingredients

1 tbsp madras curry paste
1 onion, chopped
2 carrots, diced
75g potato, diced
250g taste the difference minced beef
400g can chopped tomatoes
1.2 litres fresh beef stock
freshly ground black pepper

### Ingredients for garnish

2 tbsps chopped coriander

### Method

1. Sizzle the paste in a large saucepan with the onion for 3 minutes until softened. Add the carrots and potatoes and cook for a further 5 minutes.

2. Add the beef and increase the heat, sear well. Now add the tomatoes and stock. Season with pepper and simmer gently for 30 minutes.

3. Process half the soup until smooth and return it to the saucepan, stir well. Check the seasoning and ladel into bowls. Serve garnished with chopped coriander.

## Bacon and Butternut Soup

Serves: 4
Preparation time: 15 minutes
Cooking time: 20 minutes

### Ingredients

1 tbsp olive oil
1 onion, chopped
200g bacon - back, streaky or middle , cut into cubes

450g butternut squash, peeled, deseeded and chopped
2 carrots, peeled and chopped
750ml vegetable or chicken stock
freshly ground black pepper
3 tbsps Greek yoghurt
20g flat leaf parsley, chopped

## Method

1. Heat the oil in a saucepan, add the onion and 150g of bacon. Cook for 6-8 minutes until golden, stirring occasionally. Add the butternut squash and carrots with the stock.

2. Bring to the boil and simmer gently for 20 minutes, until the vegetables are tender.

3. Meanwhile, fry the remaining bacon for 5 - 6 minutes, and set to one side. Place the soup in a blender or food processor and blend until smooth. Season to taste.

4. Serve with the yoghurt spooned on top and sprinkle over the parsley with the crispy bacon 'croutons'.

## Oxtail Soup

Serves: 4
Preparation time: 15 minutes
Cooking time: 250 minutes

## Ingredients

25g beef dripping
1 oxtail, chopped
1 large onion, chopped
1 carrot, chopped
1 celery stick, chopped
2.25 litres beef stock
bouquet garni
1 tbsp cornflour blended with 2 tbsps water
2 tbsps sherry
freshly ground black pepper

## Oxtail Soup/cont.
### Method
1. Melt the dripping in a pan, add the oxtail and fry until well browned. Remove from the pan, add the vegetables and saute until soft. Return the oxtail to the pan, add the stock, bouquet garni and pepper. Bring to the boil, cover and simmer very slowly for 3 to 4 hours until tender.

2. Strain the soup. Remove the meat from the bones, shred finely and set aside with the vegetables. Cool the liquid, chill and skim off fat layer and return the meat and vegetables to the soup.

3. Stir in the blended cornflour and simmer, stirring for 2 minutes. Add the sherry and check the seasoning.

### To freeze
Prepare the soup to step 2. Cool the soup and spoon into a rigid container, seal, label and freeze. Thaw completely and complete as step 3.

## Lentil and Turkey Soup
Serves: 4
Preparation time: 15 mins
Cooking time: 50 mins

### Ingredients
1 x 150g pack turkey rashers
2 tbsps sunflower oil
1 small onion, finely diced
1 medium carrot, chopped
1 garlic clove, crushed
1/2 tsp chilli powder
175g/6oz red lentils
1 medium potato, peeled and chopped
1 litre/1 3/4 pints vegetable stock
200g can chopped tomatoes
1 tbsp tomato puree
1 tbsp dried thyme
1 tbsp chopped parsley and chives

## Method

1. Chop half of the turkey rashers and stir over a medium heat for 3 mins in a large pan with the onion and carrot. Add the garlic and chilli powder and cook for a further minute.

2. Place the lentils in a sieve and rinse under cold water. Add to the pan with the potato, stock, tomatoes, tomato puree and thyme. Cover and simmer for 30-40 mins until the lentils are tender.

3. Meanwhile, grill the remaining turkey rashers and cut into small pieces. Cool the soup slightly then puree in a blender or food processor.

4. Return the soup to the pan, add the chopped turkey rashers and season according to taste. Mix the parsley and chives together, scatter over the soup and serve.

## *Pea and Ham Soup*

Serves: 4
Preparation time: 15 min
Cooking time: 1 hr 5 min

### Ingredients

1 tbsp butter
2 onions, finely chopped
1 garlic clove, finely chopped
small handful of thyme leaves
800g frozen peas
1 ham bone
1 litre vegetable, pork or chicken stock

### Method

1. Heat the butter in a large saucepan over a medium heat and add the onions, garlic, thyme and peas. Cook for 3-4 minutes, stirring constantly.

2. Add the ham bone and stock. Bring to the boil and simmer for 1 hour.

3. Remove the ham bone; transfer the mixture to a blender and whiz until smooth.

# Game Soup

Serves: 4
Preparation time: 10 minutes
Cooking time: 70 minutes

## Ingredients

2 tbsps vegetable oil
1 pigeon
1 onion, finely chopped
2 carrots, finely chopped
2 celery sticks, finely sliced
1 tbsp cornflour
4 mushrooms, chopped
900ml beef stock
freshly ground black pepper

## Method

1. Heat the oil in a large pan. Brown the pigeon on all sides then remove. Add the onion, carrot and celery to the pan and fry gently until lightly browned. Stir in the cornflour and cook for 1 to 2 minutes, stirring.

2. Add the mushrooms, stock and black pepper. Place the pigeon in the pan, bring to the boil, cover and simmer for about 1 hour. Remove the pigeon from the pan and cut away the meat and return it to the soup.

## To freeze

Make the soup as above. Cool completely and pour into a rigid container, seal, label and freeze. Thaw completely and then bring to the boil, cover and simmer for 10 minutes, stirring occasionally. Check the seasoning before serving.

## Butternut Squash Soup

Serves: 4
Preparation time: 20 minutes
Cooking time: 40 minutes

### Ingredients

1 butternut squash, weighing 450g
1 large onion, chopped
2 cloves garlic
1 litre vegetable stock
125ml white wine
2 sprigs of fresh thyme
1 bayleaf
1-2 tsps freshly grated nutmeg
freshly ground pepper

### Ingredients for serving

150ml soured cream
2 tbsps snipped chives

### Method

1. Peel and slice the butternut squash, discard the seeds. Put the prepared squash into a large saucepan with the onion, garlic, stock and white wine.

2. Bring the squash to the boil and add the thyme and bayleaf, season lightly and cook over a low heat for 25-30 minutes or until the squash is tender.

3. Transfer the mixture to a food processor and whiz to form a purée. Return to the rinsed out saucepan and bring back to the boil, season to taste with nutmeg and add more seasoning if needed.

4. Adjust the consistency of the soup, if necessary with a little extra stock or milk, it should be the consistency of double cream.

5. Spoon the hot soup into individual bowls, swirl some soured cream on top, and finish with a sprinkling of chives.

## Celery and Onion Soup

Serves: 4 to 6
Prep time: 5 minutes
Cooking time: 10 minutes

### Ingredients

524g can celery hearts
425g can red kidney beans
425g can French onion soup
300ml water
150ml medium sherry
grated Parmesan cheese
freshly ground black pepper

### Method

1. Drain and chop the celery hearts, reserving the liquid. Drain the kidney beans.

2. Put the onion, soup, celery hearts with their liquid, kidney beans, water and sherry in a saucepan. Heat to just below boiling point and add pepper to taste. Pour into individual soup bowls and sprinkle with Parmesan cheese to serve.

## Carrot and Courgette Soup

Serves: 4
Preparation time: 30 minutes
Cooking time: 25 minutes

### Ingredients

25g margarine
1 large onion, chopped
250g courgettes, sliced
425g carrots, chopped
125g potato, chopped
900ml vegetable stock
freshly ground black pepper

## Method

1. Melt the margarine in a saucepan and fry the onion over a medium heat for 5-10 . minutes or until it is golden and translucent.

2. Add the courgettes, carrots, potato and stock, season with pepper, and cook for 20-25 minutes or until the vegetables are soft.

3. Leave the soup to cool slightly, then purée in a blender or food processor until smooth. Return to the pan, heat through and serve.

## *Carrot and Coriander Soup*

Serves: 4
Preparation time: 15 minutes
Cooking time: 30 minutes

### Ingredients

125g red lentils
1 bay leaf
300ml water
250g carrots, sliced
150ml orange juice
450ml vegetable stock
2 tbsps chopped fresh coriander
freshly ground black pepper

### Method

1. Place the lentils in a  pan with the bay leaf and the water and bring to the boil.

2. Reduce the heat, cover and simmer for about 20 minutes until the lentils have softened. Cook the carrots in the orange juice and stock until tender. Drain the lentils if necessary and discard the bay leaf.

3. Place the lentils, the carrots and their cooking liquid in a blender or food processor and puree until smooth.

4. Stir in the coriander and season to taste with pepper. Reheat the soup and serve with fresh bread.

## Chunky Courgette Soup

Serves: 4
Preparation time: 10 minutes
Cooking time: 20 minutes

## Ingredients

3 medium size potatoes
2 leeks
600ml stock
2 celery sticks, chopped finely
4 medium size courgettes
50g Cheddar cheese, grated (optional)
salt and freshly ground black pepper

## Method

1. Peel the potatoes and wash the leeks. Chop them and cook in the well seasoned stock with the celery until they are tender. Liquidise.

2. Cut the courgettes in half lengthways and then cut across into chunks. Simmer in the puree until cooked through but still crisp. Stir in the cheese, if using and heat through until it melts.

## Celery soup with Pesto

Serves: 4
Preparation time: 15 minutes
Cooking time: 5 minutes

## Ingredients

1 tbsp olive oil
1 red onion, finely chopped
2 cloves garlic, crushed
2 courgettes, roughly diced
1 pack trimmed celery, finely sliced
300ml milk
450ml parsley and garlic or vegetable stock
1 carton fresh pesto
basil leaves

## Method

1. Heat the olive oil in a large saucepan and add the red onion. Stir-fry for 1-2 minutes and add the garlic, courgettes and celery to the pan. Cover and cook for a further 10 minutes over a medium heat.

2. Add the milk and stock and simmer covered for 20 minutes. Stir in the pesto just before serving garnished with basil

## *Carrot and Mint Soup*

Serves: 4
Preparation time: 20 minutes
Cooking time: 35 minutes

### Ingredients

25g vegetable oil
500g carrots, sliced
1 onion, sliced
1 clove garlic, crushed
1 litre vegetable stock
1 tbsp cornflour blended with 2 tbsps water
2 tsps chopped mint
freshly ground black pepper

### Ingredients for serving

mint sprigs
4 tbsps croutons

### Method

1. Melt the oil in a large pan. Add the carrots, onion and garlic and cook gently until soft. Add the stock, and pepper to taste. Bring to the boil and simmer for 25 minutes. Puree or pass through a sieve. Cool. If freezing ahead then pour soup into a rigid container, seal, label and freeze.

2. Turn into a saucepan and heat gently. Stir in the blended cornflour and bring to the boil, gently simmer and continue stirring until slightly thickened, now add the chopped mint. Garnish with mint and serve with croutons.

# Carrot and Orange Soup

Serves: 4
Preparation time: 5 minutes
Cooking time: 35 minutes

## Ingredients

2 tbsps oil
1 large onion, finely chopped
500g frozen sliced carrots
1.2 litres vegetable stock
juice and zest of 1 orange
freshly ground black pepper

## Method

1. Heat the oil in a large pan, over a moderate heat fry the onion and carrots until softened, this will take approximately 10-15 minutes.

2. Add the stock and bring to the boil, reduce the heat and simmer for 20 minutes. Remove from the heat and pour the soup into a blender along with the juice and zest of the orange. Blend until smooth.

3. Return to the heat, season and heat through, adding a little water if the consistency looks too thick. Serve with chunks of crusty bread.

# Carrot and Ginger Soup

Serves: 4
Preparation time: 15 mins
Cooking time: 30-35 mins

## Ingredients

600g of carrots peeled and chopped
2 medium onions, peeled and chopped
1 clove of garlic, peeled and crushed
3 tbsps olive oil
1 tsp powdered ginger
1 tsp medium curry powder
1 1/2 litres vegetable stock
sea salt and black pepper
pared rind of one lemon

## Ingredients for cream

1 x 200g crème fraîche
finely grated rind of one lemon
2 tsps chopped parsley
2 tsps chopped chives

## Method

1. Heat the olive oil in a saucepan and add the onions and carrots, cook for several minutes, stirring from time to time. Do not brown the vegetables.

2. Then add the garlic, ginger and curry powder and cook for a further minute. Add the stock and lemon strips to the pan, half cover the pan with its lid, and simmer gently for 20 minutes until the carrots are tender.

3. Cool slightly, then liquidise the soup until smooth. Taste and season with sea salt and black pepper. Reheat to serve.

## Method for cream

1. Stir all the ingredients together gently, or the crème fraîche will go runny, and then spoon a dollop into the middle of each bowl of soup, garnish with chives or parsley if you wish. Serve with wholemeal crusty bread.

## Clear Leek Soup with Ginger and Mushrooms

Serves: 4
Preparation time: 15 minutes
Cooking time: 60 minutes

### Ingredients

4cm piece fresh root ginger, peeled
2 tbsps olive oil
500g leeks, sliced very finely
1 1/2 litres vegetable stock
100g button mushrooms, sliced very finely

### Method

1. Bruise the piece of ginger by crushing it lightly with a pestle or heavy knife-blade, to break the fibres and release the juices while keeping the piece whole.

2. Heat the olive oil in a heavy-based saucepan, add the leeks and ginger, cover and fry over a very gentle heat for 20 minutes or until soft.

3. Add the stock and bring to the boil, then reduce the heat and simmer for 30 minutes. Season.

4. Add the mushrooms to the soup and simmer for a further 5-10 minutes. Remove the ginger before serving.

## Cream of Mushroom

Serves: 4
Preparation time: 10 minutes
Cooking time: 15 minutes

### Ingredients

50g butter
1 small onion, chopped
250g mushrooms, sliced
25g plain flour
450ml vegetable stock

## Method

1. Melt 25g of the butter in a pan. Add the onion and cook gently stirring until softened. Add the chopped mushrooms, with a little pepper.

2. Melt the remaining 25g butter in another pan. Stir in the flour and cook, stirring, for 1 to 2 minutes. Gradually stir in the stock and bring to the boil.

3. Cook, stirring for 2 to 3 minutes, then add the mushrooms and onions. Puree the soup in an electric blender or rub through a sieve. Cool.

4. To freeze, pour into a rigid container, seal, label and freeze. To serve, turn into a saucepan and heat gently until thawed. Bring to the boil, then stir in the milk and cream. Check the seasoning. Heat through without boiling. Serve garnished with the mushrooms.

## *Wild Mushroom Soup*

Serves: 4
Preparation time: 10 minutes
Cooking time: 30 minutes

## Ingredients

50g dairy free margarine
1 medium sized onion, chopped
1 clove garlic, crushed
250g mixed wild mushrooms, sliced eg. oyster, shiitake
50g plain flour
600ml vegetable stock
salt and freshly ground black pepper
2 tbsps freshly chopped tarragon
300ml soya milk

## Method

1. Melt the margarine in a large saucepan and fry the onions and garlic for 3-4 minutes until softened.

2. Add the mushrooms to the pan and fry for a further 5 minutes until tender. Stir in the flour and cook for 1-2 minutes.

## Wild Mushroom Soup/cont.

3. Gradually add the stock, stirring continuously. Stir in 1 tbsp of tarragon. Bring slowly to the boil, then reduce the heat and simmer for 10-15 minutes.

4. Allow the mixture to cool slightly, then puree in a food processor or blender. Rub through a sieve. Just before serving add the milk or cream, season and reheat, without boiling.

5. Pour into bowls and sprinkle over the remaining tarragon.

## Chestnut Mushroom & Celeriac Soup

Serves: 4
Preparation time: 10 minutes
Cooking time: 20 minutes

### Ingredients

15g butter
1 tbsp oil
1 onion, finely chopped
1 celeriac, peeled and chopped
300g chestnut mushrooms
850ml vegetable stock
425ml milk
freshly ground black pepper

### Ingredients for serving

a little fresh cream

### Method

1. Melt the butter with the oil and soften the onion Stir in the peeled and chopped celeriac and roughly chopped chestnut mushrooms.

2. Cook for 5 minutes and then pour in the chicken stock. Bring to the boil and simmer for 15-20 minutes.

3. Blend in a liquidiser and add the milk. Season well and serve hot with a swirl of cream.

## Potato and Leek Soup

Serves: 4
Preparation time: 10 minutes
Cooking time: 30 minutes

### Ingredients

25g butter
375g leeks, sliced
1 stick celery, finely sliced
375g potatoes, peeled and roughly chopped
900ml vegetable stock
142ml carton single cream

### Method

1. Melt the butter in a large pan and cook the leeks until softened but not coloured.

2. Add the celery, potatoes, stock and seasoning. Bring to the boil, then cover and simmer for 20 minutes. Puree the soup in a blender and return to the rinsed pan. Heat through, then stir in the cream and serve.

## Pumpkin Soup

Serves: 4
Preparation time: 20 minutes
Cooking time: 20 minutes

### Ingredients

675g pumpkin
100g butter
1 bay leaf
150ml milk
150ml carton of single cream
freshly ground black pepper

### Method

1. Cut the pumpkin flesh into small cubes. Heat the butter in a pan and toss the cubes in it with the bay leaf and seasoning; cook gently until they are pulpy.

## Pumpkin Soup/cont.

2. Liquidise with the milk. Add the cream, heat through, season to taste and serve with croutons of fried bread.

## Potato, Rocket and Roasted Garlic Soup

Serves: 6
Preparation time: 1 hr
Cooking time: 1 hr 5 min

### Ingredients

1 head garlic
50g butter
2 light olive oil
1 onion, finely chopped
1 leek, finely sliced
1 large potato, finely diced
750ml milk
1 lemon, juice only
75g rocket leaves, roughly chopped
3 tbsps extra virgin olive oil
salt and fresh ground black pepper

### Method

1. Preheat the oven to 180C/350F/gas 4. Using a sharp knife, cut the very top off the garlic bulb (this will make it easier to get the roasted cloves out). Place the garlic in the oven and cook for 45 minutes, until the cloves are lovely and soft.

2. Remove the garlic bulb and leave until cool enough to handle. Squeeze out the soft cloves

3. Melt the butter and olive oil together in a large saucepan. Add the onion and leek and cook for 2-3 minutes, until just beginning to soften. Add the potato and stir thoroughly to ensure the potatoes are well coated in the butter.

4. Cover the pan and cook for a further 4-5 minutes. Pour in the stock, bring to the boil, then cover and reduce the heat. Simmer for 10-12 minutes.

5. Season the soup with plenty of salt and pepper and stir in the lemon juice and roasted garlic. Blend in batches using a liquidiser or hand-held blender. Reserve a few rocket leaves to garnish the soup and add the remaining leaves to each batch of soup as you liquidise it. Pour the soup warmed bowls and drizzle over some olive oil. Add a twist of black pepper and garnish with the reserved rocket leaves. Serve with warm bread.

## Pea Soup with Coriander

Serves: 4
Preparation time: 5 minutes
Cooking time: 15 minutes

### Ingredients

2 tbsps oil
1 onion, finely chopped
1 clove garlic, finely chopped
1 tsp ground coriander
1 vegetable stock cube
600ml water
400g frozen peas
142ml carton single cream
2 tbsps fresh coriander, finely chopped
freshly ground black pepper

### Method

1. Heat the oil, cook onion and garlic until soft. Add the ground coriander and cook for 1 minute.

2. Dissolve the stock cube in 600ml boiling water and add to the pan with the peas, cook gently for 15 minutes.

3. Liquidise until a smooth puree. Season. Stir in single cream and fresh coriander just before serving.

## Creamy Split Pea and Vegetable Soup

Serves: 4

Preparation time: 10 minutes

Cooking time: 70 minutes

### Ingredients

1 tbsp vegetable oil

750g root vegetables, such as carrots, parsnips, swede, peeled and roughly chopped

125g green split peas

125g yellow split peas

3 vegetable stock cubes made up with 2.25 litres boiling water

freshly ground black pepper

### Method

1. In a large saucepan heat the oil then add the vegetables and saute for 8-10 minutes.

2. Next add the remaining ingredients, cover and bring to the boil for 10 minutes, reduce the heat and simmer for 50 minutes.

3. Transfer the mixture to a food processor and process until smooth. Return to the rinsed pan and heat through. Serve immediately with crusty bread.

## Spinach and Butter Bean Soup

Serves: 4

Preparation time: 15 minutes

Cooking time: 15 minutes

### Ingredients

1 tbsp olive oil

2 cloves of garlic, crushed

175g baby spinach leaves

211g can of butter beans

1 litre vegetable stock

lemon rind

## Method

1. Heat the oil in a pan, and gently fry the garlic. Add the spinach and butter beans with liquid from the can and 300ml of the stock. Simmer for 15 minutes, then blend, sieve, or put through a food processor.

2. Add the remaining stock and reheat. Garnish with strips of lemon rind if you like, and serve immediately.

## Leek and Potato Soup

Serves: 6
Preparation time: 10 minutes
Cooking time: 30 minutes

## Ingredients

1 1/2 tbsps oil
750g leeks, trimmed and sliced
1 clove garlic, crushed
750g floury potatoes, diced
2 vegetable stock cubes made up with 900ml boiling water
2 tbsps freshly chopped parsley
2 slices bread, cubed
40g white matured Cheddar, grated

## Method

1. Heat a tbsp oil in a large pan, add the leeks and garlic and cook over a moderate heat for 5-6 minutes until softened but not brown.

2. Add the potatoes and stock, bring to the boil and simmer for 20-30 minutes until the potatoes are tender.

3. Add most of the parsley and seasoning to taste. Meanwhile, heat the remaining oil in a frying pan and fry the bread cubes on both sides until golden.

4. Serve the soup with the crispy croutons, grated cheese and remaining parsley sprinkled over the top.

## Lentil Soup

Serves: 4
Preparation time: 20 minutes
Cooking time: 50 minutes

## Ingredients

500g brown lentils
1.4 litres vegetable stock or water
2 Bay leaves
A small bunch of finely chopped parsley
salt and fresh ground black pepper
2 tbsp olive oil
1 medium onion, chopped
1 head of garlic, chopped
2 Carrots, finely chopped
1 small tomato, chopped
Half a red pepper, chopped
2 tsp sweet paprika
1 tbsp ground cumin
50g rice
50ml Manzanilla sherry

## Method

1. Place the lentils in a large saucepan. Add the stock or water, bay leaves and parsley. Bring to the boil, reduce the heat, season with salt and freshly ground pepper and simmer, partly covered.

2. Meanwhile, heat the olive oil in a frying pan. Fry the onion gently until softened, around 5 minutes.

3. Add the garlic, carrot, tomato and red pepper. Fry gently for 5 minutes. Remove from direct heat, season with salt and freshly ground pepper, paprika and cumin.

4. Add the onion mixture and the rice to the simmering soup. Simmer the soup until the lentils are tender, around 45 minutes in all. Mix in the sherry and serve.

## Chunky Potato and Bean soup

Serves: 4
Preparation time: 10 minutes
Cooking time: 20 minutes

### Ingredients

1 tbsp olive oil
2 cloves garlic, crushed
1 carrot, diced
1 stick celery, sliced
600g waxy potatoes eg Estima, peeled and diced
400g tin mixed beans, drained and rinsed
1 tsp dried mixed herbs
1 vegetable stock cube
850ml water
2 tsps tomato purée
2 tbsps freshly chopped parsley

### Method

1. Heat the oil in a large saucepan and gently fry the garlic, carrot, celery and potatoes for 3-4 minutes. Add the remaining ingredients and boil.

2. Simmer for 10-15 minutes or until the potatoes are tender. Season to taste and sprinkle with the parsley to serve.

## Roasted Tomato Soup

Serves: 2
Preparation time: 15 minutes
Cooking time: 50-60 minutes

### Ingredients

675g/1lb 8oz cherry tomatoes
4 cloves of garlic, unpeeled
60ml/4tbsp olive oil
1 small onion, chopped
450ml/15fl oz light vegetable stock
Salt and freshly ground black pepper to taste

## Roasted Tomato Soup/cont.
### Method

1. Preheat the oven to 200°C/400F/gas 6. Place the tomatoes and cloves of garlic in a roasting dish in a single layer. Drizzle with 3 tbsp of the olive oil and roast for about 30 mins until the garlic is tender when pierced with a knife, and the tomatoes are colouring and splitting.

2. Heat the remaining tbsp of oil in a saucepan and gently fry the onion until translucent. Squeeze the garlic out of the skins and add to the onions, together with the roasted tomatoes and all the juices from the roasting pan.

3. Pour in the stock, bring to the boil and simmer, covered for 20 mins. Cool, then blend until the soup is very smooth (make sure all the tomato skins are well blended). Return the soup to a clean pan, season to taste and gently reheat.

## Rice and Tomato Soup

Serves: 6
Preparation time: 15 minutes
Cooking time: 30 minutes

### Ingredients

1 large onion, peeled and chopped finely
400g can of chopped tomatoes
1 tbsp tomato purée
50g long grain rice
900ml well-flavoured chicken or vegetable stock
25g plain flour
300ml skimmed milk
freshly ground black pepper

### Method

1. Put the onion, tomatoes and tomato purée, rice and chicken stock in a pan, and bring it to the boil. Then cover the pan, and simmer for 30 minutes.

2. Whisk the flour and milk together until smooth. Add this to the soup, season and bring to the boil again until thickened.

# Roast Pumpkin Soup with Cinnamon

Serves: 4-6
Preparation time: 20 minutes
Cooking time: 60 - 80 minutes

## Ingredients

600g peeled and seeded pumpkin or squash cut into 3cm cubes
6 tbsps olive oil
1 medium onion, thinly sliced across the grain
2 garlic cloves, thinly sliced
1/2 tsp freshly ground cinnamon
a pinch of crushed dried chilli
1 medium potato (about 150g), peeled and cut into 2cm cubes
1 litre vegetable (or chicken) stock, preferably hot
1 medium bunch (about 40g) of coriander, coarsely chopped
1–2 tsps caster sugar

## Ingredients for serving

50g unsalted butter
30g pine nuts
1/2 tsp ground cinnamon
100g Greek yoghurt, thinned with 1 tbsp milk
1/4 garlic clove, crushed to a paste with a pinch of salt

## Method

1. Preheat the oven to 220°C/425°F/Gas 7. Toss the pumpkin with 2 tbsps of the olive oil, a good pinch of salt and some black pepper and spread it out in a roasting tin. Roast for about an hour, until very soft and starting to colour.

2. About 20 minutes before the pumpkin is ready, heat the remaining oil in a large saucepan over a medium heat. Add the onion and a pinch of salt and cook for about 15 minutes, stirring occasionally, until the onion begins to turn golden. Now add the garlic, cinnamon and chilli. Fry for another minute to release their flavour, then add the potato and a little salt and pepper. Cook for 5 minutes more, taking care that the garlic doesn't burn, then add the roasted pumpkin and the stock and bring to a gentle simmer. Cook for 20 minutes or until the potato is soft.

3. Meanwhile, prepare the garnishes. Melt the butter in your smallest pan, add the pine nuts and cinnamon and fry gently until the butter begins to caramelise and foam and the pine nuts are starting to turn a very pale brown. Scrape the bottom of the pan to release any bits that are stuck and pour the pine nuts and butter into a cool bowl to stop the cooking. In another bowl, season the yoghurt with the crushed garlic and some salt and pepper.

4. With a handheld blender or in a food processor, blend the soup until smooth. Return it to the pan, stir in the chopped coriander and check for seasoning. If the soup is not sweet enough, add a little sugar. Serve with the seasoned yoghurt, warm brown butter and pine nuts on top.

## Tomato and Lentil Soup

Serves: 4
Preparation time: 15 minutes
Cooking time: 45 minutes

### Ingredients

750g ripe tomatoes
1 tbsp sunflower oil
1 large onion, chopped finely
1 clove of garlic, chopped finely
125g split red lentils
2 tbsps chopped fresh parsley
1 tbsp chopped fresh thyme or tsp dried thyme
1 tbsp chopped fresh marjoram or 5ml spoon dried marjoram
600ml vegetable stock
freshly ground black pepper
4 tbsps low fat natural yogurt

### Method

1. Scald, skin and chop the tomatoes.
Heat the oil in a saucepan on a low
heat. Put in the onion and garlic and
soften them.

2. Add the tomatoes, lentils and herbs, and stir for 2 minutes or until the tomatoes are soft. Mash them down with a fork or potato masher.

3. Pour in the stock, bring it to the boil and season. Cover the pan and simmer for 45 minutes or until the lentils are soft.

4. Serve in individual bowls with the yoghurt spooned or swirled over the top, depending on its texture.

## Tomato and Rosemary Soup

Serves: 8
Preparation time: 5 minutes
Cooking time: 30 minutes

### Ingredients

2 tbsps sunflower oil
2 onions, finely chopped
1 clove garlic, finely chopped
2 tbsps fresh rosemary leaves, roughly chopped
2 tbsps tomato puree
1 kg fresh tomatoes, cut into quarters
1 vegetable stock cube, made up to 1 litre with boiling water
2 x 410g cans cannellini beans, drained, reserving a few for garnish
freshly ground black pepper

### Method

1. Heat the oil in a large saucepan and cook the onion over a low heat until soft-ened. Add the garlic, rosemary and tomato puree and continue cooking for a further minute.

2. Place the tomatoes and stock into the saucepan, bring to the boil and then cover and simmer for 15 minutes. Add the beans and cook for another 5 minutes.

3. Blend or liquidise the soup until smooth, reheat and garnish with reserved beans and a sprinkling of black pepper. Serve with crusty bread.

## Apple and Celery Soup

Serves: 4
Prep time: 10 minutes
Cooking time: 25 minutes

### Ingredients

1 tbsp oil
1 small onion, finely chopped
1/2 x pack trimmed celery, finely sliced
2 x Granny Smith apples, peeled, cored and roughly chopped
300ml milk
300 ml vegetable stock, plus an additional 150ml water

### Method

1. Heat the oil in a saucepan and add the onion, celery and apple and cook for 5 minutes or until softened but not browned. Add the milk and stock and simmer for 20 minutes. Pour in batches into a blender and process until smooth. Return to the heat and warm through.

## Beetroot and Orange Soup

Serves: 4
Preparation time: 10 minutes
Cooking time: 10 minutes

### Ingredients for the soup

2 tbsps oil
1 onion, finely chopped
250g pack ready to eat beetroot, cut into small cubes
1 orange, zest and juice
1 vegetable stock cube made up with 600ml water

### Method

1. Heat the oil in a saucepan and cook the onion slowly until softened but not coloured.

2. Add the beetroot, orange zest and juice and stock then cook gently for 7-10 minutes. Blend or liquidise until smooth. Chill well before serving.

## Tomato and Basil Soup

Serves: 4

Preparation time: 10 minutes

Cooking time: 15 minutes

## Ingredients

1 tbsp sunflower oil

1 onion, chopped

450g pack vittoria tomatoes, cut into quarters

700g jar passata

1 vegetable stock cube

250ml water

1 - 3 tsps sugar

freshly ground black pepper

1 large pot basil, leaves torn

2 tbsps single cream

half baguette, sliced and lightly toasted

gruyere cheese, sliced

## Method

1. Heat the oil in a large saucepan over a moderate heat. Add the onion and fry for 3 minutes or until transluscent. Add the tomatoes, passata, crumbled stock cube and the water. Stir and bring to the boil, reduce to a simmer for 10 minutes.

2. Preheat the grill to a moderate heat. Pour the soup into a food processor or use a hand held blender to process until smooth. Return to the saucepan, add the sugar and seasoning to taste. Stir in the torn basil leaves and heat for 5 minutes stirring occasionally.

3. Meanwhile, top the toasted slices of baguette with slices of cheese and place under the grill for 1 - 2 minutes or until the cheese melts and bubbles. Stir the cream into the soup. Pour the soup into bowls and top each bowl with the cheese toasts. Serve immediately.

## Creamy Celery with Stilton

Serves: 4
Preparation time: 20 minutes
Cooking time: 35 minutes

## Ingredients

1 tbsp olive oil
1 onion, finely diced
2 large potatoes, diced
1 head celery, thoroughly washed and roughly chopped
1 tsp caraway seeds
1 vegetable stock, made up ith 600ml boiling water
300ml semi-skimmed milk
142ml pot single cream
75g stilton cheese, crumbled
20g pack fresh chives, roughly chopped

## Method

1. Heat the oil in a large saucepan then add the onion, potato, celery and caraway seeds, saute for approximately 5 minutes.

2. Next add the stock and milk and simmer uncovered for 20-30 minutes. Transfer the soup to a food processor and process until smooth, return to the rinsed saucepan.

3. Gently heat the soup, then stir in the single cream. Crumble the stilton cheese into individual soup bowls and top with ladles of the soup. Sprinkle with chives and serve immediately with hot crusty bread.

# *Vegetarian Baby Corn and Tofu Soup*

Serves: 4 - 6

Preparation time: 25 minutes

Cooking time: 50 minutes

## Ingredients

1 tbsp olive oil

1 tsp granulated sugar

3 shallots or 1 onion, chopped

1 garlic clove, chopped, optional

1 small dried red chilli, optional

5cm piece of fresh ginger, peeled and chopped roughly

1 medium size carrot, washed and cut into chunks

the stalks from the spinach

1.5 litres water

## Ingredients for garnish

375g baby sweetcorn, sliced thinly

200g smoked tofu, cut into 1cm cubes

10 to 12 spinach leaves or more, roughly shredded

salt and freshly ground black pepper

## Method

1. Heat the oil in a saucepan, and add the sugar. Stir for 2 minutes, then add the rest of the ingredients for the stock, except the water.

2. Stir these around for 2 minutes and then add the water. Bring to the boil and simmer for 30 to 40 minutes.

3. Strain the stock into another saucepan, and discard the solids. This stock can be prepared well in advance.

4. About 10 minutes before you are going to serve the soup, heat the clear stock until it is just boiling, and add the baby corn and smoked tofu.

5. Let this simmer for 6 to 8 minutes, adjust the seasoning, and add the spinach. Leave the soup to simmer for 10 seconds, and serve immediately.

# Vegetable Soup

Serves: 4
Preparation time: 10 minutes
Cooking time: 25 minutes

## Ingredients

50g butter
150g peeled potatoes, cubed into 2cm pieces
1 large onion, peeled and chopped
375g chopped, peeled vegetables, ie carrots, parsnip and celery
freshly ground black pepper
2 vegetable stock cubes, made up with 1 litre boiling water
150ml full fat milk

## Method

1. Melt the butter in a saucepan, when hot add the potatoes, onion and vegetables, stir to coat in the butter.

2. Sprinkle with pepper, then cover and sweat on a low heat for 10 minutes. Add the stock and bring to the boil then simmer until the vegetables are soft, this will take approximately 5 minutes.

3. Liquidize, add the milk and adjust the seasoning. Serve as suggested.

# Tuscan Bean Soup

Serves: 4
Preparation time: 10 minutes
Cooking time: 20 minutes

## Ingredients

2 tbsps olive oil
2 celery sticks, chopped
1 red onion, sliced thinly
2 carrots chopped
2 courgettes, chopped
432g can of canellini beans, drained and rinsed
250g smoked pork sausage, cut into 2.5cm lengths
500g jar or carton of passata
salt and freshly ground black pepper
To serve: grated parmesan cneese

## Method

1. Heat the oil in a large saucepan and fry the celery, onion and carrots for 5 minutes until they start to soften. Add the courgettes and cover the pan and cook gently for a further 5 minutes.

2. Add the beans, sausage and passata and bring slowly to simmering point. Cook for a further 10 minutes. Season to taste. Ladle the soup into deep soup bowls and sprinkle with Parmesan cheese.

# Vermicelli Soup

Serves: 4
Preparation time: 10 minutes
Cooking time: 45 minutes

## Ingredients

2 tbsps cooking oil
125g vermicelli
1/2 onion, quartered
1 clove garlic, skewered on a cocktail stick
4 sprigs parsley

## Vermicelli Soup/cont.

2 whole chillies
1.2 litres chicken stock
3 tbsps tomato purée
50g parmesan cheese
1 tbsp chopped parsley

## Method

1. Heat the oil in a large frying pan and fry the vermicelli until it is golden brown - this happens very quickly. Remove the vermicelli with a slotted spoon and drain on absorbent paper.

2. Remove all but 1 tbsp of oil and fry the onion and garlic until golden. Add the reserved vermicelli, parsley, chillies, stock and tomato purée. Stir well. Cover and simmer for 15 minutes; then uncover and cook for a further 30 minutes, stirring occasionally.

3. When the mixture starts to dry out, it is ready to serve. Discard the onion, garlic, parsley and chillies. Serve sprinkled with the parmesan cheese and chopped parsley.

## Quick Chicken Noodle Soup

Serves: 4
Preparation time: 5 minutes
Cooking time: 10 minutes

## Ingredients

900ml chicken stock
240g pack 2 roast chicken breasts, skin removed and finely shredded
50g capelli d'angelo pasta, cut into 1cm pieces
freshly ground black pepper
20g pack flat leaf parsley, finely chopped

## Method

1. Place the stock in a saucepan and bring to simmering point. Add the chicken and cook for 4 minutes, adding the pasta for the final 2 minutes of the cooking time.

2. Season to taste with freshly ground black pepper then finish with parsley. Serve immediately with chunks of crusty bread.

## Ricotta Soup

Serves: 4
Preparation time: 20 minutes
Cooking time: 30 minutes

### Ingredients

2 tbsps olive oil
1 large onion weighing about 200g chopped
325g ricotta cheese
200g fresh spinach or swiss chard, shredded
2 ripe tomatoes, skinned and chopped
1 tbsp chopped fresh parsley
750ml water
4 small slices of bread, toasted
freshly ground black pepper

### Ingredients for serving

2-3 tbsps freshly grated parmesan or pecorino cheese

### Method

1. Heat the oil in a saucepan, add the onion and fry over a low heat for about 5 minutes or until soft but not brown.

2. Add the ricotta, increase the heat and cook, stirring and mashing the ricotta with a wooden spoon.

3. When it starts to brown and stick to the bottom of the pan, add the spinach or chard, tomatoes, parsley and enough water to cover. Season and bring to the boil, then reduce the heat and simmer for 15 minutes.

4. Put a slice of toast in the bottom of four individual serving bowls and ladle over the soup. Top with the grated cheese and freshly ground black pepper.

## Pancetta and Bean Minestrone

Serves: 4
Preparation time: 20 minutes
Cooking time: 75 minutes

## Ingredients

1 tbsp olive oil
130g pack pancetta
2 medium sized onions, chopped
1 clove garlic, crushed
1 red pepper, deseeded and finely chopped
1 green pepper, deseeded and finely chopped
350g courgettes roughly chopped
2 tbsps tomato purée
1.2 litres chicken stock
75g conchigliette pasta
200g canned cannelini beans
1 tbsp chopped fresh thyme
1 tbsp chopped fresh marjoram
4 tbsps chopped fresh parsley
freshly ground black pepper
freshly grated parmesan cheese

## Method

1. Heat the oil in a large saucepan, add the pancetta, onions, garlic and peppers. Cook until soft and add the courgettes, tomato paste and the stock.

2. Season, lower the heat and cook gently for 10 minutes. Add the pasta and beans and cook for a further 8-10 minutes or until the pasta is cooked.

3. Add the herbs, serve in big, deep bowls and sprinkle with freshly grated Parmesan cheese.

## Florentine Potato Soup

Serves: 4
Preparation time: 10 minutes
Cooking time: 40 minutes

### Ingredients

1 kg potatoes, peeled
1 litre water or vegetable stock
500g ripe tomatoes, chopped
1/2 large or 1 small onion, chopped finely
1 carrot, chopped finely
1 celery stick, chopped finely
a small handful of fresh parsley and basil, chopped
5-6 tbsps extra virgin olive oil
crusty bread

### Method

1. Put the potatoes in a large saucepan with the water or stock. Bring to the boil and cook for 8 minutes, then add the tomatoes, onion, carrot, celery and herbs.

2. Reduce the heat, cover and simmer until the potatoes have turned to pulp. Remove the soup from the heat, leave to cool slightly, then push through a food mill or sieve into a large bowl.

3. Return the soup to the saucepan and season to taste, then stir in the olive oil and heat through briefly, without cooking the oil.

Serve hot with plenty of crusty bread.

## Red Onion Soup with Cheese Toast

Serves: 4
Preparation time: 10 minutes
Cooking time: 1 hr 20 minutes

## Ingredients

30ml/2 tbsp sunflower oil
15g/1/2oz butter
650g/1 lb 7oz small red onions, peeled and thinly sliced
10ml/2 tsps sugar
15ml/1 tbsp plain flour
10ml/2 tsps wholegrain mustard
1.2 litres beef or vegetable stock
2 large sprigs fresh thyme
8 thin slices French bread
50g/2oz Gruyère cheese
Fresh thyme leaves, to garnish

## Method

1. Heat the oil and butter in a large deep pan. Add the onions and cook gently over a low heat for 10 minutes, stirring frequently. Sprinkle over the sugar and cook for a further 10 minutes until the onions are soft.

2. Stir in the flour and mustard, and cook for 1 minute. Add the stock and thyme sprigs and season well with salt and freshly ground black pepper. Bring to the boil, then reduce the heat to a simmer and cook for 30-40 minutes.

3. Lightly toast the slices of French bread and top with the cheese. Return to the grill for 1-2 minutes until the cheese melts.

4. Remove the thyme sprigs from the soup. Ladle the soup into deep bowls and top each with 2 cheese toasts. Serve immediately, garnished with thyme leaves.

## French Onion Soup

Serves: 4
Preparation time: 30 minutes
Cooking time: 60 minutes

## Ingredients

6 tbsps butter
10 onions, chopped
50g plain flour
1 tbsp tomato purée
50ml white wine
1 litre chicken stock
100g Gruyère, grated
4 slices french bread, toasted

## Method

1. Melt the butter in a large saucepan over a low heat and cook the onions for 30 minutes until softened, stirring constantly.

2. Add the flour, tomato puree, wine and chicken stock. Cook for a further 30 minutes. Season to taste with salt and freshly ground black pepper.

3. Scatter the grated cheese over the toasted French bread slices and grill until the cheese is golden and bubbling.

4. Serve the soup immediately, with a piece of cheese topped toast floating on the top of each.

## *Minestrone*

Serves: 4
Preparation time: 30 minutes
Cooking time: 30 minutes

## Ingredients

2 sticks of celery, sliced
1 onion, finely chopped
2 rashers of streaky bacon, rind removed
2 tbsps virgin olive oil
1 carrot, peeled and finely sliced
2 cloves of garlic, crushed
1 leek, sliced
100g white cabbage, shredded

## Minestrone/cont.

3 tomatoes, peeled, de-seeded and chopped
1 litre chicken stock
50g cooked haricot beans

## Method

1. Cook the celery, onion and bacon in the olive oil until beginning to brown. Add the carrot, garlic, leek, cabbage and tomatoes and continue frying for a further 4-5 minutes.

2. Add the chicken stock, bring to the boil and simmer for 25 minutes or until all the vegetables are cooked.

3. Add the haricot beans and season to taste with pepper, bring to the boil and simmer for a further 10 minutes.

4. Serve in a large soup tureen with the Parmesan cheese separately.

## Meatball Minestrone

Serves: 4
Preparation time: 15 minutes
Cooking time: 40 minutes

## Ingredients

15ml/1 tbsp olive oil
1 large leek, trimmed and sliced
225g/8oz carrots, peeled and diced
600ml/1 pint vegetable stock
500g carton passata with garlic and herbs
1 large courgette, diced
350g packet Swedish-style meatballs

## Method

1. Heat the oil in a large deep pan. Add the leek and carrots and fry for 5 minutes. Pour in the stock, bring to the boil, then reduce the heat to a simmer and cook for 15 minutes.

2. Add the passata and courgettes and season well with salt and freshly ground black pepper. Simmer for a further 15 minutes until the vegetables are tender.

3. Stir in the meatballs and cook for 5-6 minutes until heated through. Adjust the seasoning to taste, then serve in warmed bowls with crusty bread.

## Roasted Pepper and Tomato Soup with Meatballs

Serves: 6-8
Preparation time: 15 minutes
Cooking time: 45 - 60 minutes

### Ingredients

750g/1lb 10oz large ripe tomatoes
4 red peppers
4 shallots, halved
30ml/2tbsps virgin olive oil
15ml/1 tbsp dried
pinch Italian seasoning
225g/8oz lean finely minced beef
Few fresh basil leaves
5ml/1 tsp garlic purée
10ml/2 tsps tomato purée
300ml/1/2 pint vegetable stock
5ml/1tsp sugar
fresh basil leaves, to garnish

### Method

1. Preheat the oven to 200°C/400°F/Gas 6. Score a cross in the top and base of each tomato and place in a roasting tin with the peppers, shallots, olive oil and Italian seasoning.

2. Season with salt and freshly ground black pepper and roast for 20-25 minutes until the tomatoes are soft, with charred, peeling skins, and the peppers are blistered and blackened skins.

3. Carefully place the hot peppers in a plastic bag and leave until cool. Leave the tomatoes and shallots to cool in the roasting tin.

## Roasted Pepper and Tomato Soup with Meatballs/cont.

4. To make the meatballs, place the minced beef, basil leaves, garlic and tomato purée in a food processor or blender. Season well and process for a few seconds. Shape into 20 mini meatballs. Place in a small roasting tin and cook in the oven for 20 mins, turning once.

5. Peel the peppers, discarding the seeds and pith, and remove the skins and any tough core from the tomatoes. Place both in a food processor or blender with the shallots and any juices from the roasting tin. Process until smooth. You may need to do this in 2 batches.

6. Transfer the pepper and tomato mixture to a large pan and stir in the vegetable stock and sugar. Heat through gently and adjust the seasoning to taste. Serve with the meatballs and garnish with fresh basil.

## Haricot and Caldos Verdi Soup

Serves: 4-6
Preparation time: 10 minutes
Cooking time: 20 minutes

### Ingredients

1 tbsp olive oil
1 shallot, finely chopped
1 clove garlic, finely chopped
1 potato, cut into 0.5cm cubes
15g pack fresh leaf parsley, roughly chopped
1/2 savoy cabbage, shredded
1.2 litres vegetable stock, (made up with 2 stock cubes)
410g can haricot beans, drained and rinsed
salt and freshly ground black pepper

### Method

1. Heat the oil in a heavy based pan. Gently fry the shallot and garlic for 1-2 minutes. Stir in the potato and parsley and fry for a further 2 minutes.

2. Stir in the cabbage and stock, stir well. Bring to the boil, then reduce the heat and simmer for 15-20 minutes. Add in the haricot beans for the final 10 minutes. Season to taste and serve with crisp croutons.

## Creamy Flageolet Soup

Serves: 4
Preparation time: 5 minutes
Cooking time: 30 minutes

## Ingredients

25g butter
1 medium onion, chopped
2 medium leeks, sliced
200g flageolet beans, soaked overnight and cooked as pack instructions
600ml vegetable stock, made up with 1 stock cube
4 tbsps creme fraiche
freshly ground black pepper
1 tbsp fresh parsley, chopped

*Flageolet beans, the caviar of beans, are tiny, tender French bush type beans that are very popular in French cooking. If you can't find them, substitute haricot beans instead.*

## Method

1. Melt the butter in a large saucepan and cook the onion and leek gently for 10 minutes.

2. Add the flageolet beans and stir for a minute before adding the stock. Bring to the boil and simmer gently for 15 minutes.

3. Liquidise the soup, return to the pan and stir in the creme fraiche. Season to taste. Reheat gently but do not boil. Serve with a sprinkling of parsley.

# Dutch Edam, Haddock, Mussel and Bacon Chowder

Serves: 4-6
Preparation time: 10 minutes
Cooking time: 25 minutes

## Ingredients

150ml/1/4 pint wine (or water if preferred)
500g/1lb 2oz fresh mussels, cleaned and checked (optional)
1 tbsp olive oil
115g/4oz rindless, streaky bacon, chopped
1 onion, finely chopped
1 garlic clove, crushed
600ml/1 pint vegetable stock
500g/1lb 2oz potatoes, peeled and cubed
350g boneless, skinless haddock fillet, cut into small chunks
75ml/3 fl oz double cream
150g/5 1/2 oz frozen peas or petit pois
115g/4oz Edam cheese, cut into small cubes
3 tbsps fresh chives, chopped

## Method

1. Place the mussels in a large pan, pour over the wine (or water if preferred), cover and cook for approximately 4 minutes until all the mussels are open. Drain and reserve the liquid. When cool enough to handle remove the mussels from their shells.

2. Heat the olive oil in a large pan and cook the bacon for 3 minutes. Add the onion and cook until softened, about 6 minutes. Stir in the garlic and cook for a further minute.

3. Pour in the stock and reserved mussel liquid and bring to the boil. Add the potatoes and simmer for 8 minutes. Stir in the haddock and cook for a further 3 minutes.

4. Pour in the cream, petit pois, mussels and warm through. Stir in the Edam and chives and season to taste. Pour into warm serving bowls and serve with crusty bread.

# Cauliflower and Swiss Emmental Soup

Serves: 4-6
Preparation time: 5 minutes
Cooking time: 20 minutes

## Ingredients

60g/2oz unsalted butter
1 onion, finely chopped
1 leek, finely chopped
1 carrot, peeled and finely chopped
1 bay leaf
1 large cauliflower, cut into small florets
1 litre/1 3/4 pints vegetable stock
2tbsp thyme leaves, plus extra sprigs to garnish
150ml/5 fl oz double cream
125g/4 1/2oz Emmental, grated
100g/3 1/2oz Goat's Cheese log, rind removed and crumbled

## Method

1. Melt the butter in a saucepan and add the onion, leek, carrot and bay leaf. Cover and cook gently for 2-3 minutes, until the vegetables begin to soften. Do not let them brown. Add the cauliflower florets and cook gently for a further 4-5 minutes.

2. Pour in the stock, bring to the boil, then reduce the heat and simmer for 15-20 minutes, until the cauliflower is very tender. Stir in the thyme leaves.

3. Purée the soup in a blender until smooth and return to the saucepan and bring just to the boil. Whisk in the cream and Emmental.

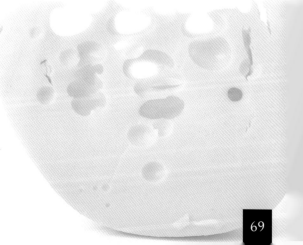

4. Season with nutmeg, salt and pepper and then ladle into bowls. Scatter a little of the goat's cheese over each soup and garnish with thyme and a little more black pepper.

# Italian Cauliflower Soup with Cheese Croutons

Serves: 6
Preparation time: 15 minutes
Cooking time: 35 minutes

## Ingredients

1 large cauliflower
1 white potato, diced
750ml whole milk
1 litre vegetable stock, hot
Bunch of spring onions, thinly sliced
25g butter
25g plain flour
100g Grana Padano, coarsely grated, plus extra

## For the cheese croutons

2 thick slices country bread
1-2 tbsps olive oil
2 tbsps finely grated Grana Padano
1 garlic clove, crushed

## Method

1. Break the cauliflower into even-size florets and place in a large pan with the potato, milk, stock and the white part of the spring onions (reserve the green part).

2. Bring to the boil and simmer for 20 minutes, until the cauliflower is very soft. Strain the liquid into a jug. Set aside the vegetables.

3. Heat the butter in a large pan, add the flour and cook for 1 minute, stirring frequently. Gradually beat in the reserved hot liquid to make a smooth sauce. Bring to the boil and simmer for a further 2-3 minutes.

4. Add the cheese and stir until melted. Add the vegetables and some salt and pepper and purée using a hand-held blender, until smooth.

Alternatively, transfer to a food processor, in batches, and whizz until smooth. Keep warm.

5. Meanwhile, make the croutons. Preheat the oven to 190°C/375°F/Gas 5. Cut the crusts off the bread and discard. Cut the bread into cubes and toss with the olive oil, cheese, garlic and season to taste. Scatter onto a baking sheet and bake for 10 minutes, until crisp and golden.

6. Ladle the soup into bowls and scatter with the reserved spring onions. Top with the extra cheese, croutons and black pepper.

## Italian-style Bean Soup

Serves: 1
Preparation time: 10 minutes
Cooking time: 20 minutes

### Ingredients

1 tbsp olive oil
1 small onion, peeled and chopped
1 clove garlic, peeled and crushed
227g can chopped tomatoes
1/2 tsp dried oregano
220g can kidney beans, drained and rinsed
300ml (1/2pt) vegetable stock
75g (3oz) green beans, topped, tailed and halved
Salt and freshly ground black pepper
1 ciabatta roll, sliced open
2 tbsps pesto sauce

### Method

1. Heat the oil in a small saucepan and gently fry the onion and garlic for 4 - 5 mins until softened but not browned. Stir in the tomatoes, oregano and kidney beans. Bring to the boil, cover and simmer very gently for 10 mins.

2. Meanwhile, pour the stock into another small saucepan and bring to the boil. Add the green beans, cover and cook for 5 mins until just tender.

3. Add the cooking stock along with the cooked beans to the tomato mixture. Stir well, season and keep warm over a low heat while preparing the toasts.

## Italian-style Bean Soup/cont.

4. Preheat the grill to hot. Line the grill tray with foil and arrange the ciabatta on the foil. Cook under the grill for 2 - 3 minutes until lightly toasted. Spread with pesto sauce and grill for a few seconds longer until piping hot.

5. Ladle the soup into a warm bowl and eat immediately with the toasted pesto ciabatta.

## White Bean Soup with Pistou

Serves: 4
Preparation time: 5 minutes
Cooking time: 30 minutes

### Ingredients

2 tbsps oil
1 onion, finely chopped
1 clove garlic, finely chopped
2 medium size tomatoes, skinned and deseeded
1 medium carrot, cut into fine dice
1 medium parsnip, cut into fine dice
1 medium potato, cut into fine dice
1 stick celery, cut into fine dice
1 leek, cut into rings, then into 4
2 vegetable stock cubes made up with 1.25 litres of water
420g can white haricot beans
1 tbsp fresh thyme, finely chopped
1 tbsp fresh coriander, finely chopped

### Ingredients for the pistou

1/2 x 15g pack fresh basil, finely chopped
3 cloves garlic, finely chopped
2 tbsps olive oil
50g parmesan, freshly grated (optional)

Pistou sauce, or just pistou, is a cold sauce made from cloves of garlic, fresh basil, and olive oil. Some more modern versions of the recipe include grated parmesan, pecorino or similar hard cheeses.

Traditionally, the ingredients are crushed and mixed together in a mortar with a pestle, (pistou means pounded in the Provençal language).

## Method for soup

1. Heat the oil in a large saucepan, add the onion and garlic then cook until softened.

2. Add the other fresh vegetables and allow them to cook gently for 3-4 minutes. Add the vegetable stock and cook for 30 minutes.

3. Add the white beans and herbs 10 minutes before the end.

## Method for pistou

1. Crush and mix together the basil, garlic, olive oil and parmesan with a mortar and pestle.

2. Place this mixture into the base of the soup tureen, or a little in the base of each soup bowl and pour the soup over the top.

73

## Chorizo and Baby Leaf Curly Kale Soup

Serves: 2-3
Preparation time: 10 minutes
Cooking time: 20 minutes

## Ingredients

120g baby leaf curly kale
100g chorizo, chopped
1 large potato, cubed
1 onion, finely chopped
1 red pepper, cut lengthways
1 garlic clove, crushed
250ml water
1 tbsp olive oil
Salt and pepper

## Method

1. Heat olive oil in a large deep pan, add the garlic, onion, red pepper and potato. Fry gently for 2-3 minutes.

2. Add 250ml water, cover and simmer vigorously on a medium heat for 15 minutes or until potato is soft. Dice the potato.

3. Add the baby leaf curly kale and cook through until the baby leaf curly kale is wilted and soft. Season and serve.

# Vietnamese Beef and Spinach Soup

Serves: 4

Preparation time: 30 minutes

Cooking time: 5 minutes

## Ingredients

450g fresh spinach, stalks removed

175g lean fillet steak, cut into thin slices about 5cm long

2 Shallots, finely sliced

3 garlic clove, finely chopped

3 tbsps Fish Sauce

freshly ground black pepper

1.2 litres chicken stock

1 tbsp lemon juice

1 tsp sugar

1 small red chilli, deseeded and chopped

## Method

1. Bring a large pan of salted water to the boil and blanch the spinach leaves for a few seconds until they are just wilted. Drain well and refresh in cold water to prevent further cooking. Drain again, squeezing out excess water.

2. Combine the steak strips with the shallots, garlic, 1 tbsp of fish sauce and a grinding of black pepper, and then set aside.

3. Just before you are ready to eat, bring the chicken stock to a simmer in a large saucepan and stir in the remaining fish sauce, together with the lemon juice, sugar and chilli.

4. Stir in the blanched spinach and the beef, with its marinade.

5. Bring the soup back to simmering point; add another good grinding of black pepper and serve at once.

## Spicy Beetroot and Coconut soup

Serves: 6
Preparation time: 10 minutes
Cooking time: 50 - 55 minutes

### Ingredients for soup

500g raw beetroots
2 tbsps vegetable oil
2 banana shallots, finely chopped
1 tsp cumin seeds
600ml vegetable stock
400ml coconut milk
1 pinch sea salt

### Ingredients for paste

2 lemon grass stalks
2 garlic cloves, peeled
3 red chillies
5 cm fresh ginger root, peeled
4 kaffir lime leaves
1 lime, juice

### Ingredients for serving

1 tbsp fresh mint
1 tbsp coriander leaves
Small cucumber, chopped, deseeded

### Method

1. Preheat the oven to 200C/400F/Gas 6. Sprinkle the beets with 1 tbsp of vegetable oil and season with sea salt. Wrap them in kitchen foil, place in a roasting tray and roast for 35 minutes until tender. Cool, peel and chop.

2. For the paste, peel the tough outer coating from the lemon grass stalks. Finely chop the white bulbous part of each stalk, discarding the rest.

3. Put the lemon grass, garlic, chillies, ginger, kaffir lime leaves and lime juice in a blender. Blend until smooth.

4. Heat the remaining vegetable oil in a saucepan. Add the shallot and cumin seeds and fry gently for 2-3 minutes.

5. Add half the paste and fry for 5 minutes, stirring now and then, until fragrant. Add the roast beetroot and fry for 2 minutes. Pour in the stock, bring to the boil and simmer for 7-8 minutes.

6. Just before serving, put the soup, coconut milk, and the remaining paste in a blender and blend until smooth.

7. Top with chopped mint, coriander and cucumber and serve immediately.

## Chinese Beef Broth

Serves: 4
Preparation time: 15 minutes
Cooking time: 15 minutes

### Ingredients

50g fine egg thread noodles
1 tbsp olive oil
1 red onion, sliced
1 tbsp fresh chopped ginger
1 red chilli, deseeded and chopped
100g button mushrooms, finely sliced
1.2 litres fresh beef stock
100ml dry sherry
50g mangetout
100g baby sweetcorn, finely chopped
3 tbsps soy sauce
300g sirloin steak, finely sliced

### Ingredients to garnish

2 tbsps chopped fresh coriander

### Method

1. Boil a kettle of water and pour over the noodles. Set aside whilst preparing the soup.

## Chinese Beef Broth/cont.

2. Heat the oil in a wok and add the onion, ginger and chilli. Stir fry for 2 minutes. Throw in the mushrooms and stir fry for a further 3 minutes. Pour in the stock and sherry. Simmer for 5 minutes.

3. Add the mangetout, sweetcorn and soy sauce. Simmer for 3 minutes. Drain the noodles and add to the soup with the finely sliced beef. Stir and simmer for 3 minutes. Ladle into bowls and serve garnished with coriander.

## Thai Lemon Chicken Soup

Serves: 4
Preparation time: 10 minutes
Cooking time: 30 minutes

### Ingredients

1 tbsp vegetable oil
250g chicken breast, sliced thinly
1/2 tsp turmeric
1/2 tsp red chilli, chopped
150ml coconut milk
1 chicken stock cube, made up with 600ml water
2 tbsps lemon juice
2 tbsps crunchy peanut butter
3 spring onions, sliced
1 tbsp fresh coriander, chopped
1 tbsp desiccated coconut
freshly ground black pepper

### Method

1. Heat the oil in a large pan and fry the chicken, turmeric and chilli powder for 3-4 minutes.

2. Stir in the coconut milk, chicken stock, lemon juice and peanut butter. Cover and simmer for 15 minutes.

3. Add the spring onions, coriander and seasonings and cook for a further 5 minutes. Serve the soup sprinkle with desiccated coconut.

## Chilli Prawn Noodle Soup

Serves: 4
Preparation time: 15 minutes
Cooking time: 10 minutes

### Ingredients

100g rice noodles
1 tbsp vegetable oil
1 medium onion, finely chopped
2 spring onions, roughly chopped
1 clove garlic, finely chopped
2 tsps medium curry powder
1 green chilli, finely chopped
2 lemon grass stems, crushed
15g coriander stalks, crushed
75g creamed coconut
400ml water
200g raw tiger prawns, shelled
500ml chicken stock
50g spinach leaves
4 tsps Thai fish sauce, nam pla
2 tbsps coriander, roughly chopped

### Method

1. Cook the noodles following pack instructions and refresh under cold water. Heat the oil in a saucepan and fry the onion, spring onion, garlic, curry powder and chilli for 1-2 minutes.

2. Add the lemon grass, coriander, creamed coconut, water, prawns and stock and simmer for 5 minutes.

3. Add the spinach leaves, and nam pla and simmer for a further minute. Before serving add the chopped coriander, and remove the lemon grass and coriander stalks.

# Cauliflower and Coconut Soup

Serves: 6
Preparation time: 15 minutes
Cooking time: 30 minutes

## Ingredients

2 tbsps sunflower oil
1 onion, finely chopped
1 large carrot, diced
250g cauliflower florets
1 cooking apple, peeled, cored and diced
1/2 tsp each of ground cumin, coriander, turmeric and ginger
1/4 tsp chilli powder
1 litre vegetable stock
50g creamed coconut
3 tbsps freshly chopped coriander
410g can borlotti beans, drained
salt and freshly ground black pepper

## Method

1. Heat oil in a saucepan, add the onion and carrot and saute gently for 5 minutes. Add the cauliflower florets, apple and spices and cook for a further 1-2 minutes.

2. Add the stock, bring to the boil, cover and simmer for 20 minutes.

3. Stir in the remaining ingredients and simmer gently until the coconut has melted.

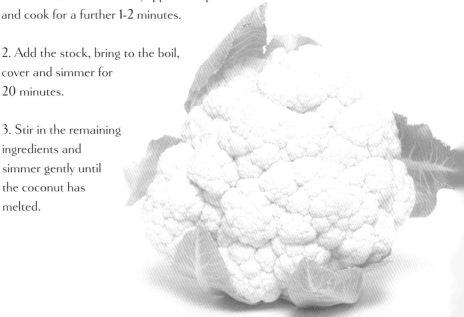

# Chicken, Coconut and Coriander Soup

Serves: 4

Preparation time: 15 minutes

Cooking time: 10 minutes

## Ingredients

1 tbsp vegetable oil

1 onion, finely diced

2 skinless chicken breast fillets, finely sliced

2 chicken stock cubes made up to 900ml with boiling water

juice of 1/2 x lemon

75g creamed coconut

large pot coriander

freshly ground black pepper

## Method

1. Heat the oil in a saucepan, add the onion and chicken and cook over a moderate heat for 5 - 6 minutes, stirring occasionally until cooked through but not browned.

2. Add the stock, lemon juice and creamed coconut. Bring to the boil and simmer for 1 minute. Add the coriander and seasoning to taste. For extra heat, try adding some finely chopped fresh chilli to the onion before cooking.

As an alternative, add a stick of fresh lemon grass, split instead of the lemon juice. For a really luxurious flavour, use 3 x 300ml tubs fresh chicken stock instead of the stock cubes and water.

## Chicken Laksa

Serves: 4
Preparation time: 10 minutes
Cooking time: 15 minutes

## Ingredients

1 tbsp sesame oil
2 skinless chicken breasts, cut into strips
1 tsp fresh root ginger, peeled and finely chopped
1 garlic clove
2 tsps green curry paste
2 Thai green chillies, deseeded and finely chopped
100g green beans, trimmed and cut in half
1 small courgette, cut into batons
1 spring onion, sliced on an angle
200ml coconut cream
1/2 x chicken stock cube made up with 150ml boiling water
1 tbsp fish sauce
1 tbsp soy sauce
1 bundle rice noodles, cooked as per pack instructions and refreshed
juice of 1 lime
20g pack fresh coriander, finely chopped

## Method

1. Heat the oil in a large frying pan or wok and cook the chicken strips for 5-6 minutes or until cooked through, remove and put to one side.

2. Add the ginger, garlic, green curry paste and chillies and cook for 1 minute. Add the green beans and cook for a further minute.

3. Return the cooked chicken and add the courgette, spring onion, coconut cream, stock, fish sauce and soy sauce. Simmer over a low heat for 3-4 minutes, or until the vegetables are tender and the chicken is warmed through.

4. Take four individual serving dishes and divide the noodles between them. Add the lime juice to the soup base then pour over the noodles. Finish with some coriander and serve immediately.

## Thai Chicken Soup

Serves: 4
Preparation time: 10 minutes
Cooking time: 35 minutes

## Ingredients

1 chicken carcass, weighing approximately 375g
2 pieces of lemon grass
2 lime leaves (optional)
1 small green chilli, chopped
2 small red chillies, chopped
1 medium size onion, unpeeled and quartered
2 x 175g skinless, boneless chicken breasts, chopped or shredded
juice of 1 1/2 limes

## Method

1. Place the chicken carcass in a large saucepan with 1 piece of lemon grass, 1 lime leaf if using, the chillies and onion. Cover with 1.2 litres water and bring to the boil. Reduce the heat and simmer for 30 minutes.

2. Remove the pan from the heat and allow the stock to become completely cold. Strain the stock, then chill overnight. The next day, remove the fat from the surface of the stock.

3. Return the stock to the saucepan, add the chicken, the remaining lemon grass and lime leaf if using, and bring to the boil. Reduce the heat and add the lime juice. Simmer for 10 minutes until the chicken is cooked.

4. Spoon the chicken into individual soup dishes and pour over the stock. Serve immediately.

## Thai Chicken, Prawn and Noodle Soup

Serves: 4
Preparation time: 10 minutes
Cooking time: 10 minutes

### Ingredients

2 x 500g packs ribbon noodles in Thai style curry sauce
500ml chicken stock
4 salad onions, finely sliced
200g pack baby corns and mange tout, sliced lengthways
2 cooked chicken breasts, shredded
100ml coconut milk

### Method

1. Cook the noodles following the pack instructions. Stir in the sauce and the chicken stock, cook for 1 minute. Add the remaining ingredients and combine. Gently pour into a large bowl and serve immediately.

## Thai, Green Curry Chicken Soup

Serves: 4
Preparation time: 5 minutes
Cooking time: 10 minutes

### Ingredients

1 tbsp oil
4 tbsps Thai green curry paste
250g chicken breast, cut into fine strips
400ml chicken stock, fresh or made up from a stock cube
200ml coconut cream
15g pack coriander leaves, chopped
juice of 2 limes

### Method

1. Heat the oil in a saucepan, add the Thai green curry paste and cook over a gentle heat for 5 minutes. Add the chicken and cook until browned. Add the chicken stock and coconut cream, bring to the boil and simmer for 7 minutes. Add the chopped coriander leaves and lime juice.

## Dhal Soup

Serves: 6-8
Preparation time: 5 minutes
Cooking time: 90 minutes

### Ingredients

500g pack yellow split peas (soaked overnight and drained)
1.75 litres chicken stock
1 head of garlic, chopped
1/2 teaspon ground tumeric
16 cloves
2cm piece ginger, peeled and sliced thinly
26 black peppercorns, tied in cheesecloth with the cloves
salt and freshly ground black pepper

### Ingredients for serving

creme fraiche
naan bread

### Method

1. Place the split peas in a large pan. Add the stock, garlic, ginger and turmeric, and the peppercorns and cloves tied in cheesecloth.

2. Boil for 10 minutes, then reduce and cook for a further hour or so until the peas are tender.

3. Remove the garlic head and cheesecloth, and season to taste. Pass the soup through a strainer (spooning hard), or blend in a processor. Reheat gently and serve with a spoonful of creme fraiche and naan bread.

## Coconut and Chicken Soup

Serves: 4

Preparation time: 20 minutes

Cooking time: 15 minutes

## Ingredients

400ml vegetable stock

3 pieces galangal, finely sliced

6 kaffir lime leaves

4 stalks lemongrass, finely sliced

4 coriander root or 20 stems

6 shallots

2 small green chilli

400ml coconut milk

200g sliced chicken breast

1 tbsp fish sauce

1 tbsp sugar

3 tbsps tamarind juice

2 tbsps lemon juice

2 tbsps chilli oil

## Method

1. Put the stock in a pan and bring to the boil. Add the galangal, Kaffir lime leaf, lemongrass, crushed coriander, shallot and chilli, Simmer for 1 minute, then add the coconut milk and continue to simmer for another 1-2 minutes.

2. Add the chicken or tofu, fish sauce, sugar, tamarind and lemon juice - if using chicken, leave to simmer until cooked through.

3. Bring back to the boil, then remove from the heat and serve in a dish topped with the chilli oil.

# Morrocan Harira

Serves: 8
Prep time: 10 minutes
Cooking time: 60 minutes

## Ingredients

250g chicken, preferably from the leg, diced
250g chick peas, soaked for 1 hour
1 onion, coarsely chopped
250g tomatoes, skinned and chopped
3 litres chicken stock
1 tsp ground cinnamon
125g rice or vermicelli
a bunch of fresh coriander or parsley, finely chopped
3 medium eggs, beaten
2 lemons, cut into wedges
freshly ground black pepper

## Method

1. Put the chicken, chick peas, onion and tomatoes to boil in the stock. Remove any scum.

2. Add the pepper and cinnamon, then simmer for about 1 hour until the chick peas are soft.

3. Fiffteen minutes before you want to serve, add the rice or vermicelli. Finally add the coriander or parsley, take the soup off the heat and beat the eggs in vigorously - they will cook enough to thicken the soup.

Serve hot with lemon wedges.

## Mulligatawny Soup

Serves: 4
Preparation time: 5 minutes plus overnight soaking
Cooking time: 65 minutes

### Ingredients

225g split yellow peas soaked overnight in water
1 tbsp vegetable oil
1 onion, chopped
1 apple, cored and chopped
5cm piece root ginger
1 tbsp medium curry paste
900ml vegetable stock
100g bag of watercress

### Method

1.  Drain the soaked peas and set aside. Heat the oil in a large pan, add the onion and apple and sauté for 4 minutes until softened. Add the ginger and curry paste and stir in the peas. Stir well.

2. Add the stock, bring to the boil, cover and simmer for 1 hour.

3. Transfer to a food processor, add the watercress and blend until the soup is fairly smooth. Season to taste and serve with crusty bread.

## Prawn and Coconut Soup

Serves: 4
Preparation time: 5 minutes
Cooking time: 10 minutes

### Ingredients

chicken stock cube made up with 600ml water
400ml can coconut milk
2 stalks fresh lemon grass, cut into 2cm pieces
6 kaffir lime leaves, torn into quarters
2cm piece root ginger, peeled and thinly sliced
200g uncooked tiger prawns

1 tbsp fresh coriander, chopped
1 red chilli, sliced
2 tbsps lemon juice
salt and freshly ground black pepper

## Method

1. Pour the chicken stock and coconut milk into a pan. Add the lemon grass, lime leaves and ginger. Bring to the boil.

2. Add the prawns and boil for 3-4 minutes until cooked. Remove from the heat and add the coriander, chillies and lemon juice. Season to taste.

## *Thai Fish Soup*

Serves: 4
Preparation time: 10 minutes
Cooking time: 20 minutes

## Ingredients

2 sticks lemon grass, sliced
3 red chillies, de-seeded and chopped
1/2 tsp turmeric or 1 tsp chopped fresh turmeric
4 kaffir lime leaves
1/2 tsp coriander seeds
2 1/2cm piece galangal or ginger, peeled and chopped
1 tbsp peanut oil
1 litre shellfish stock
4 spring onions, finely chopped
2 tbsps fish sauce
110g Chinese cabbage, finely sliced
juice of 1 lime
225g cooked and peeled prawns
1 tbsp Thai basil
freshly ground black pepper

## Method

1. Put the lemon grass, chili, turmeric, lime leaves, coriander seeds and galangal into a food processor. Pound together to form a paste.

## Thai Fish Soup/cont.

2. Heat the oil in a large frying pan, add the paste and stir fry over a low heat, add the stock and simmer over a low heat for 20 minutes.

3. Strain the stock into a clean saucepan add the spring onion, fish sauce and cabbage, simmer over a low heat for 7-10 minutes or until the cabbage is tender.

4. Add the lime juice, kaffir leaves, cooked prawns and basil to the stock, heat for 2-3 minutes or until the prawns are very hot. Season to taste with pepper and serve very hot.

The cooked prawns will harden and toughen if heated for too long - add them at the very last minute, but make sure that they are piping hot when served.

# Shiitake Noodle Soup

Serves: 4

Preparation time: 10 minutes

Cooking time: 15 minutes

## Ingredients

1 tbsp sesame oil

1 tbsp cornflour

4 tbsps mirin

1 tbsp light soy sauce

1 medium size egg white

2 chicken breasts, cut into 1cm strips

120g pack shiitake mushrooms, sliced

3 salad onions, sliced diagonally into 1cm pieces

200g pack soba noodles, cooked as per pack instructions and refreshed

2 chicken stock cubes made up with 900ml boiling water

## Ingredients for serving

2 tbsps chilli sauce

## Method

1. In a large frying pan or wok heat the oil over a moderate heat.

2. In a bowl combine the cornflour, 2 tbsps of the mirin, a tsp of the soy sauce and the egg white. Then coat the chicken strips and fry for 4-5 minutes or until cooked.

3. Next add the mushrooms and spring onions and cook for a further 3-4 minutes. Finally add the stock, the remaining mirin and soy sauce, heat through for 2-3 minutes.

4. Divide the noodles between the serving bowls and pour the soup on top. Spoon a little chilli sauce into the centre of each bowl of soup and serve immediately.

## Oriental Turkey Soup

Serves: 4
Preparation time: 15 minutes
Cooking time: 15 minutes

## Ingredients

1.2 litre chicken stock
125g cooked turkey, cut into thin strips
1 bunch salad onions, sliced diagonally
1 red pepper de-seeded and sliced into thin strips
175g oyster mushrooms, roughly chopped
75g bamboo shoots
2cm piece fresh root ginger, finely grated
2 tbsps dry sherry
2 tbsps dark soy sauce
salt and freshly ground black pepper
1 tbsp freshly chopped coriander

## Method

1. Place the stock in a large saucepan and bring to the boil. Add the turkey, salad onions and pepper, simmer for 2 minutes.

2. Stir in the mushrooms, bamboo shoots, ginger, sherry, soy sauce and simmer for 2 minutes.

3. Add the seasoning to taste and simmer for a further 1-2 minutes. Sprinkle over the coriander and serve.

Shiitake Noodle Soup, pp 91

Smoked Cod Chowder, pp 21

Smoky Corn Chowder, pp 24

Smoked Haddock Sweetcorn Chowder, pp 23

Spiced Beef Soup, pp 26

Spicy Beetroot and Coconut Soup, pp 76

Spicy Carrot Soup, pp 16

Spicy Leek Soup with Blue cheese, pp 13

Spicy Marrow Soup, pp 14

Spicy Red Pepper Soup, pp, 15

Spicy Tomato Chowder, pp 18

Spinach and Butter Bean Soup, pp 44

Split Pea and Vegetable Soup, Creamy, pp 44

Sweetcorn and Prawn Soup, pp 20

Thai Chicken Soup, pp 83

Thai Chicken, Prawn and Noodle Soup, pp 84

Thai Fish Soup, pp 88

Thai, Green Curry Chicken Soup, pp 84

Thai Lemon Chicken Soup, pp 78

Tomato and Basil Soup, pp 53

Tomato and Lentil Soup, pp 50

Tomato and Rosemary Soup, pp 51

Tomato and Rocket Pesto Soup, Chilled, pp 10

Tomato Chowder, Spicy  pp 18

Tomato Soup, Roasted, pp 47

Tuscan Bean Soup, pp 57

Vegetable Soup, pp 56

Vegetarian Baby Corn and Tofu Soup, pp 55

Vermicelli Soup, pp 57

Vietnamese Beef and Spinach Soup, pp 75

Watercress Soup /cheese croutons, Chilled, pp 9

White Bean Soup with Pistou, pp 72

Wild Mushroom Soup, pp 39

## Sample Conversions

| | Cup | Grams | Ounces |
|---|---|---|---|
| Almonds - shelled, whole | 1 | 150g | 5oz |
| Almonds - chopped/flaked | 1 | 75g | 3oz |
| Almonds - ground | 1 | 150g | 5oz |
| Aubergine/Eggplant - raw - diced/chopped | 1 | 250g | 9oz |
| Apples  - sliced | 1 | 175g | 6oz |
| Apples -  chopped/diced | 1 | 100g | 4oz |
| Apricots - fresh/raw - sliced | 1 | 225g | 8oz |
| Apricots - fresh/raw - chopped/diced | 1 | 150g | 5oz |
| Apricots - cooked - chopped/diced | 1 | 75g | 3oz |
| Apricots - dried | 1 | 150g | 5oz |
| Asparagus - fresh/raw - cut in pieces | 1 | 125g | 5oz |
| Asparagus - tinned/cooked - cut in pieces | 1 | 175g | 6oz |
| Aubergine/Eggplant - raw - diced/chopped | 1 | 250g | 9oz |
| Avocado - fresh - cubed | 1 | 1 medium | 1 medium |
| Bacon - raw - chopped/diced | 1 | 225g | 8oz |
| Baking Powder | 1 | 180g | 6oz |
| Bananas - fresh/raw - sliced | 1 | 225g | 8oz |
| Bananas - fresh/raw - chopped/diced | 1 | 200g | 7oz |
| Bananas - fresh/raw - mashed | 1 | 300g | 11oz |
| Beans - All - dry | 1 | 200g | 7oz |
| Beans - Black, Kidney - cooked | 1 | 62g | 2.5oz |
| Beans - Lima, Navy - cooked | 1 | 75g | 3oz |
| Beans - Green/French/Runner - fresh/raw | 1 | 150g | 5oz |
| Beans - Green/French/Runner - cooked | 1 | 180g | 6oz |
| Bean sprouts | 1 | 100g | 4oz |
| Beef - raw - minced/ground | 1 | 225g | 8oz |
| Beef - cooked - chopped/diced | 1 | 150g | 5oz |
| Beetroot/Beets - raw - sliced/diced/grated | 1 | 150g | 5oz |
| Beetroot/Beets - cooked - sliced/diced | 1 | 200g | 7oz |
| Black/Redcurrants | 1 | 100g | 4oz |
| Blueberries/Bilberries - fresh/raw | 1 | 100g | 4oz |
| Bread - fresh/stale - broken into pieces | 1 | 50g | 2oz |
| Breadcrumbs - Fresh | 1 | 50g | 2oz |
| Breadcrumbs - dry | 1 | 90g | 3.5g |